The Journey to
Hangtown Haven

The Journey to
Hangtown Haven

ARTHUR A EDWARDS

Kravitz & Sons
INNOVATORS IN PUBLISHING, MARKETING AND ADVERTISING

Kravitz and Sons LLC
1301 Farmville Blvd, Suite 104
Greenville, NC 27834

Published by Kravitz and Sons LLC.
ISBN: Softcover   979-8-89639-064-0
           eBook   979-8-89639-063-3

Library of Congress Control Number: 2024927537

Table of Contents

AUTHOR'S PREVIOUS NOVELS:

War is Hell — Robertson Publishing

> A novel about war, its effect on the participants and a soldier's search for meaning.

A Hero's Life — Robertson Publishing

> A story of an aerospace engineer who discovers a design flaw in his country's prime fighter plane and must decide whether to blow the whistle on it and take it out of service or say nothing and let them continue to crash.

DEDICATION

Dedicating this story is easy. It is dedicated to the millions of homeless people in our great country whose lives have fallen into unimaginable despair through no fault of their own. It is also dedicated to those brave Americans who are willing to donate their time and finances to help these folks get back on their feet in spite of organized resistance from wealthy neighbors. It is especially dedicated to our returning veterans who cannot assimilate back into American society and who live on the streets searching for peace and personal identity.

A special thanks goes to my schoolteacher wife, Shirley, who would much rather have spent her time enjoying her retirement than reading and correcting her husband's book. It would not exist if it were not for her.

"There comes a time when silence is betrayal and the truth must be told."

— Martin Luther King

"There is no justification for lack of housing."
"Homeless people walk in the footsteps of Christ."

— Pope Francis

"We shall pass this way on earth but once, if there is any kindness we can show, or good act we can do, let us do it now, for we may never pass this way again."

— Dan Blocker

"Anti-homeless ordinances are cruel and unusual punishment, violating the 8th amendment of the U.S. Constitution. Criminalizing homelessness is both unconstitutional and misguided public policy. In addition, until there is enough housing, anti-camping ordinances also violate the 8th amendment of the U.S. Constitution as cruel and unusual punishment."

Federal Department of Justice (August 2015)
Bell v City of Boise

The Los Angeles' ban on living in vehicles was struck down by the 9th U.S. Circuit Court of Appeals on Thursday, removing a tool used by the city to regulate homeless persons. LA cannot seize abandoned personal gear left by homeless people on the streets.

9th Circuit Court of Appeals

Search for justice! Help the oppressed.
Hear the orphan's plea.
Defend the widow.

Isaiah 1: 17

I was hungry and you gave me food.
I was thirsty and you gave me water.
I was a stranger and you welcomed me.
I was naked and you gave me clothing.
I was sick and you took care of me.
I was in prison and you visited me.

So when you hold out your hand selflessly,
And give help to the stranger in need,
Then whatever you do for the least of mine,
You do for me.
— Matthew 25-35, 40

To practice virtue is to selflessly offer assistance to Others,
giving without limitation of one's time, Abilities, and
possessions in service, whenever and Wherever needed,
without prejudice concerning the Identity of those in need.

The character of your existence is determined By the energies
to which you devote yourself. What you do is what you are.

Who can enjoy enlightenment and remain indifferent to the
suffering in the world.
— Lao Tzu

INTRODUCTION

This book describes the work that a group of volunteers did in the planning, designing, building and operating a successful homeless shelter in El Dorado County. Along the way it describes, after retiring from a calm, secluded life in the gold country of California, the author's transition into a leader who directed the effort to create a shelter for the homeless population in his community. He learned lessons in collaboration and cooperation while battling the local power and political elite as they continually tried to shut down the shelter.

The story brings together the lives of several homeless men and women whose paths crossed on their journey through Hangtown Haven, their new home shown on the cover. It shows that it is possible for people, with a little help, to work their way out of homelessness and desperate poverty and back into the middle class community, a trip that many people in society believe is impossible.

It also includes a description of how the author, a retired aerospace engineer, affected their lives and how the homeless learned that they each had hidden skills, talents and capabilities that blossomed while living in the homeless community called Hangtown Haven, in Placerville, California. They discovered that the synergy of their efforts working together was far greater than the sum of each one's talents individually.

Also, this book details ways that non-profit corporations can be successful in helping the poor and homeless in their communities. It outlines what is legal and what is illegal in providing shelter and sustenance to poor, homeless people who have lost their homes and who are facing a life of drug abuse and alcohol addiction.

All of the stories and interviews are true, and all the conclusions reached by the author are based on real events. There is an old saying in the Navy that, "All safety rules are written in blood." Although one homeless woman died during this journey, the volunteers usually did not have to deal with blood. Nevertheless, the homeless in El Dorado County were, and are, subjected every day to events that certainly affect their lives and safety.

It also disproves many beliefs and conclusions often outlined and put into print by professionals who have written articles describing the behavior of disadvantaged people. The volunteers found that, "Homeless people are just like the rest of us. They just don't have a place to sleep." They also found that people tend to react the way you expect them to. When the shelter residents were given responsibilities and a few tools for their own survival, they responded magnificently. This book also touches on the lives of the lives of volunteers, churches, individuals and non-profit organizations that helped when funding and political muscle were needed.

Unfortunately, the ultimate fate of Hangtown Haven was determined by the political and financial power in the community that operates behind the scenes and exercises control beyond the public's knowledge. The good news is that the fight is not over by a long shot. This is a period of pause, a time of reflection, re-grouping and planning. It is a time to review what the volunteers did and apply their experiences to build another successful, this time permanent, facility to house the homeless in our community.

Please remember as you read this, that each homeless person faces the reality of survival every day of his or her life. It is easy to criticize a person's behavior without acknowledging the fact that the food he stole or the illegal place where he is sleeping results in one more day of life for that person. What would you do if your life were on the line?

The book includes biographical chapters, letters and reports throughout the story while introducing the reader to several of the volunteers and homeless residents who the author met during the past ten years.

Our memories sometimes play tricks on us and the author's is no exception. He has made every attempt to verify and confirm the events outlined herein, but he makes no guarantee that everything stated is absolutely as it happened. Dates are the toughest. He apologizes if you find an error in the story.

The author has interspersed his feelings and beliefs periodically. They are all based on his experiences both as an aerospace engineer and as a pioneer in trying to help the homeless. You may agree with them or not as you see fit. This book would not be complete without the expression of his beliefs and the causes for events as the author sees them. He is only human and has developed strong feelings for the homeless and disadvantaged in our society beginning during the depression. He, nevertheless, hopes that you, and homeless who read it, will enjoy this true story.

The homeless are still with us. Ignoring them does not make them go away. City and county governments spend millions of dollars on dog shelters, baseball parks and basketball stadiums but nothing to help our homeless neighbors. There are marches and "runs" to raise money for cancer and other worthy causes. It is now time to face the homeless situation in our communities head-on and commit appropriate energies and funds to alleviate their suffering. Mathew 25:40 quotes Christ as saying:

"What you do for the least of mine you do for me."

Whether we are Christian, Jew, Muslim, Buddhist or Atheist, how long are we going to ignore Christ's teaching?

CHAPTER ONE

Autobiography

Art Edwards

I was born in the month that my dad called the financial bottom of the Great Depression, June of 1932. I have since learned from reading history books that the actual bottom of the depression was in July, but I never corrected my dad. He liked to say that things started looking up for the country the month I was born. I am an only child.

We survived the depression pretty well as both my parents worked, my dad as a construction company plant superintendent and my mother as a junior high school music teacher. We lived in East Oakland not far from Mills College.

Things took a turn for the worse when my dad lost his job in 1938 and we had to live on my mother's salary alone, maybe $100 a month or less. Fortunately, dad went to work at the Naval Supply Center in Oakland when defense spending began to pick up in 1940. Two years later he was promoted to the job of base superintendent at the Naval Fuel Depot at Point Molate in Richmond, California. In 1953, he moved to Alameda

to become Superintendent of Public Works at the Naval Air Station where he was working when he died in 1962.

My dad was convinced that I should become an engineer, a naval officer, and attend Annapolis to do both. He had spent three years in the Navy shortly after the end of World War I, (the Great War), was a commissioned naval officer during W W II and thought his son should eventually serve his country also as an engineer and an officer. Consequently, he took me to work with him whenever I was not in school. As a result, I grew up around construction equipment, welding work, shop tools and machinery of all kinds. Naturally I became interested in how they all worked. "You can only know that when you become an engineer," he would remind me.

By the time I was twelve years old, I had definitely decided to be a mechanical engineer. I read everything I could about how automobile and aircraft engines worked and how turbines and rockets operated, at least to the extent that was known in the 1940's. I was fascinated by pumps and how refrigerators got things cold, how automobiles were designed and why airplanes stayed in the air (Bernoulli's equation); how large ships could keep from sinking of their own weight (Archimedes). Naturally I was going to be a mechanical engineer if I could get through Cal's engineering school. That turned out to be much more difficult than I had thought.

As my dad had hoped, I applied to enter Annapolis to become a naval officer when I graduated from high school and received an appointment to the class entering in 1951. However, I turned the appointment down much to my dad's chagrin. I joined the Naval ROTC at Berkeley instead and became both a naval officer and an engineer. I graduated in 1954, spent two years on an attack troop transport mostly in Korea and then returned to civilian life and went to work in the aerospace business at Lockheed Missiles and Space Company in Sunnyvale.

My career at both Lockheed and later at Ford Aerospace centered on one very important aspect of satellite development, the operational testing of completed space craft in the environment of outer space. It was (and is) called "space simulation testing." I helped design and build the first and largest space chambers at companies around the country. The first large space chamber built in the world was one that I designed at Lockheed in 1960 and was called the HIVOS Chamber (High Vacuum Orbital Simulator). It was eighteen feet in diameter by twenty-five feet long and was the first vacuum chamber in the world that would hold a fully assembled satellite.

From there I went on to help build other space chambers around the country. I was the field engineer on the large chamber at McDonnell Douglas in Huntington Beach, California, installed the vacuum pumps on the space flight simulator at the Johnson Space Flight Center in Huston Texas, (the one the astronauts trained in) and helped finish up the space chamber at NASA, Greenbelt, Maryland.

When I returned to Lockheed I designed and built three more large space chambers and then transferred to Ford Aerospace where I supervised the operation of their large space chamber. Needless to say, most of the satellites we tested were highly classified, and my security clearance was above top secret.

In the process of working in the space industry, I obtained a masters degree in cybernetic systems and began part-time teaching in some of the colleges in our area. I taught engineering and business management courses at the University of California at Santa Cruz, Cal State at San Jose, Adult Education in San Jose and Organizational Behavior at The University of San Francisco in Santa Clara County for twelve years.

I also became a classical musician at age thirteen and played the timpani in the Oakland Symphony Orchestra, Santa

Cruz Symphony, Chapman Symphony, Sierra Symphony and others. I was the youngest player in its history in the Oakland Symphony when I first started playing in 1946.

In 1994 my school-administrator wife and I retired to El Dorado County. At first I did some consulting work in my field of expertise but soon decided that I would rather kick back and go fishing. I soon found out that that was an idle dream.

We joined Federated Church (Presbyterian and Methodist) in Placerville and became somewhat active in the activities in the community. One evening my wife announced that we were going to church to hear a short presentation by a member of a local non-profit organization, United Outreach. She said that the speaker was looking for volunteers to help in their work with the homeless.

There were perhaps a dozen or so people sitting around the table at church that night to listen to the president of United Outreach, a man by the name of Raj Rambob, tell us about their commitment to helping the homeless in our community. He told us about the Seventh Day Adventist Church in Camino, up the hill from Placerville, that was providing a shelter for the homeless several nights a week. They needed volunteers to bring snacks and sit with the homeless in the evenings, talk and play cards.

In spite of shaking my head while jabbing my wife in the ribs, I couldn't keep her from raising her hand, "We will do one night." So began my twelve-year struggle to provide a permanent shelter for the members of our homeless community.

CHAPTER TWO

Meeting The Homeless

It was the summer of 2006. "So tell me again why we are doing this?" I asked my wife while driving east on Highway 50 in a not-too-goodmood. "It's not like we don't have anything else to do."

"Yes it is, dear. Plus they want help in sheltering the homeless. You need to meet them and get to know each one. I'm sure your attitude will change once you do. Besides didn't your mother tell you something about always helping those in need during the depression," my wife replied.

"So, let my mother do it."

"Don't be such a grump. Besides, your mother is probably looking down from heaven and smiling on you right now."

We later learned that United Outreach and the Camino Seventh Day Adventist Church had combined initially to use their Placerville school for a homeless shelter. They had guaranteed that all of the homeless would be out of the school when the children arrived in the morning. The school board initially approved the plan, but when the parents heard about it, they raised such uproar that the school changed its mind, and the shelter was moved to the Camino church.

A similar situation had occurred about twenty years before when the Placerville City Council authorized the city to purchase the Hangtown Haven Motel on Upper Broadway and turn it into a permanent homeless shelter. It all went well until the public got wind of the deal and a large group of them complained to the council, which cancelled the deal. That was apparently the last time the city attempted to spend any money to help the homeless.

The Camino Church was housing the homeless in its gymnasium, a building separate from the church sanctuary. As we walked in that first night, I saw about thirty- five homeless men and women scattered around the gym, some at tables eating, some playing cards and others sitting around on their sleeping bags reading and talking with each other. Several volunteers were circulating among the group making conversation and playing cards, dominoes and cribbage. "Let's go up to that table and introduce us to those homeless over there," my wife said. That was the beginning of a long relationship.

Pastor Craig Klatt had organized this sleepover for two nights a week in conjunction with Raj, the President of United Outreach. They had rounded up volunteers from various churches in the county and ten to twelve people came each night, some spending the entire night sleeping on the floor with the homeless.

Some of the homeless were transported to and from the church from Placerville on the local transit bus and some by volunteers in their cars. They were not allowed to smoke in the gym or drink alcoholic beverages anywhere on the property. This latter point was not easy to enforce. The scheduled volunteers provided snacks and a quick morning breakfast, and the rest of us were there to keep the visitors occupied and happy. The first of our responsibilities was to get to know them.

"So what did you do before you became homeless?" My wife looked over and scowled at me.

"What my husbands means is, tells us about your life growing up." Engineers are not trained in making conversation, so I had to rely on my schoolteacher wife to break the ice. I do have to admit that I learned many things from the homeless men and women we got to know. Even my reluctance to make conversation faded away.

One of the most interesting young men I met over the years was a veteran who had just returned from Iraq. By now I had learned how to encourage the homeless to talk about themselves and share their feelings with strangers.

He, I will call him Bill, was a man in his early twenties and had been a Marine Corps sharpshooter. He said that he had just returned and had been discharged only a few weeks ago but could not acclimate himself to civilian life. Consequently he became homeless and was living on the streets of Placerville. I asked him to tell me about being a sharp shooter. First I asked him what kind of weapon he had fired. "A fifty caliber rifle," he replied.

"Wow! That must kick like a mule."

"Oh yea. It would set me back a few feet each time I fired it and I always had a sore shoulder. I could, and did, kill the enemy over a thousand yards away from me, and they never knew what hit them. They couldn't even see me.

"Judging the wind's effect on the bullet was the biggest problem because the wind would change direction several times after the bullet left my weapon and before it reached the target. But I got pretty good at it. Not many of us who started sharpshooter school were able to finish. It takes a certain skill, a calmness and ability to concentrate."

Having been a gunnery officer in the Navy, I was pretty familiar with the various weapons in use during the Korean War, and had fired a fifty-caliber machine gun in training, but I had never heard of a fifty-caliber rifle. My shoulder would feel it when I fired my thirty-caliber deer rifle. My mouth must have dropped open as he continued.

"There were two of us working together as a team, my spotter and I. He sat beside me looking through high-powered binoculars and advising me on windage and deflection. The

image that appeared in my scope was electronically transferred to his binoculars, so he could see exactly what I was looking at."

"So why did you leave the Marine Corps?" I asked innocently.

"Because I got tired of killing people."

I couldn't think of anything else to say, but I could see why he was having trouble adjusting to civilian life.

We had an unusually high number of veterans in our homeless community, some from as far back as the Vietnam War. I wish I had taken the time to hear all of their stories.

Bill finished up, "We all owe you guys in the Korean War a vote of thanks because many of the weapons we used were developed by you back in the fifties. They were there for us and saved our lives because we learned to use them very well."

I wasn't sure I deserved or wanted any credit for that, but I was very happy that Bill had survived and come home, even if he was homeless on the streets of Placerville.

One of the more important questions I have for our society is why we send young men and women off to foreign countries to fight our wars and then let veterans return to a life of homelessness and addiction? Of course not all veterans return to homelessness, but enough do that we should take note and do something about it.

I have known a number of veterans who suffer the unimaginable stress of going into battle. When I was still a kid, a young Army veteran of W W II who had just returned from fighting in Italy spent hours trying to explain to me how he felt about killing men and being shot at in return. My conclusion after listening to this stressed young man was that we who haven't done it will never understand. He had what we today would call PTSD and would probably spend the rest of his life with it.

I guess that the perceived problem is that if we did something to house our veterans, especially those with PTSD, we would also have to provide shelters for the rest of the homeless. Society would rather leave veterans to sleep on the street than provide a shelter for everyone. It is easier to ignore the problem than to help those who need it

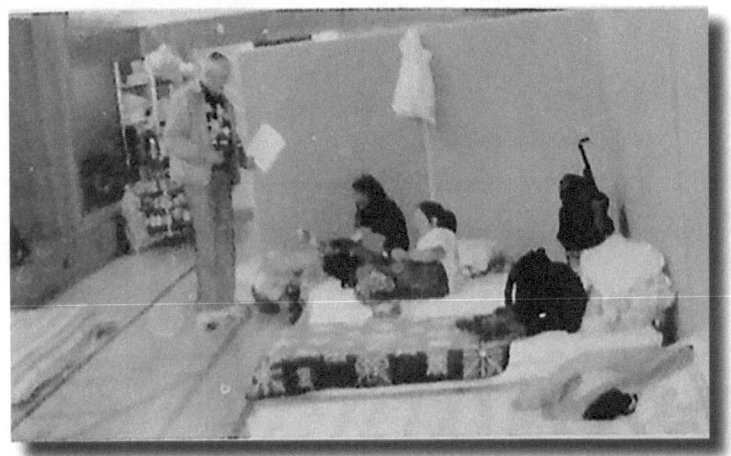

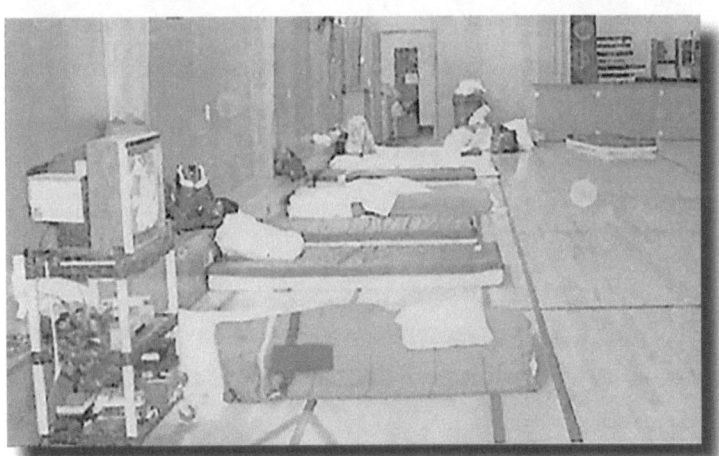

**Pastor Craig Klatt With Homeless
Sleeping at The Camino Church**

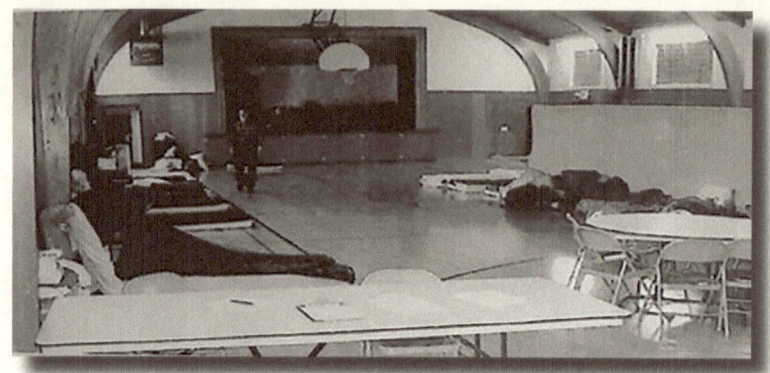

The Gym

Volunteers Preparing Snacks

CHAPTER THREE

Ron S.

I met Ron in 2006 while we were working together at the homeless shelter in the Camino Seventh Day Adventist Church. He also attended the United Outreach board meetings that were open to the public. I soon became impressed with his experience, knowledge and most of all, his dedication to helping the homeless.

Ron Sachs attributes his ministry to homeless persons from his early life living as an outsider," "the newcomer," "the odd kid out" wherever his family went. During his schooling in Germany, France or within the U.S., he found that the "street people" were always accepting even though they were the "outsiders" of their communities. Ron rather naturally seemed to fit in with this group and had resources that those who were marginal or "without" did not have. He saw their needs and has responded to those needs throughout his lifetime.

Where did his eventual journey with Jesus and the homeless begin? He learned to live the life of a rebellious art student in the streets of Chateauroux in Paris, France, but his journey started at the knee of an understanding and talented mother who instilled the wonders and curiosity of life in him and showed him what having faith can accomplish.

He arrived in Chateauroux after just one year of high school in the U.S. and found himself to be an "outsider" at that school. He "did not belong" and was falsely accused of cheating by a teacher. After demonstrating that it could not have been him, he was referred to by students and teachers as a cheater. He was sometimes beat up by the "football gang". He was not welcome with other students and was definitely a "loner". His other high school years were spent in Germany at an American school

but not with the military kids. The "army brats" had their own cliques and camaraderie, and he was not one of them.

From this he learned to do "his own thing" some of which raised eyebrows. He spent a day and a half in the Chateauroux lock-up, a dungeon. Yes he admits that he did something wrong, but his father thought it might make an impression on him to spend some time in jail. It was a great learning experience that he has remembered all his life.

After Chateauroux he broke a few rules in the Air Force, and lost his flying wings due to "dangerous flying tendencies" He was eventually honorably discharged as an Airman 2nd class.

Coming to California at 46 in 1980 and starting a new career, a new life and a new adventure, he looked forward to business and retirement. In 1986 he began attending a fundamentalist community church. This rekindled an interest in biblical research that started while he was in his artist mode searching for the "Truth." He had been brought up as a Methodist instilled with a curiosity and desire to question.

He ventured into the Unitarian belief and preached in that faith while all the time experiencing other religions as he discovered them. Yes, he has some "strange" religious beliefs that range from belief in nothing, to belief in everything.

While attending a fundamentalist church and attending Bible class, he began to serve in a church sponsored prison ministry which was headed by a gentle giant, who, although he was a fearsome sight to behold, was a "real man" in the earthly sense, and was a "real man" in the Christian since. He lived his life as if Jesus was always at his shoulder.

While Ron was volunteering in the prison ministry in 1988, at age 54 he became homeless himself after a divorce and the loss of his business. He moved into his truck. He says that he needed that experience, that complete loss of income, self-esteem, with

nowhere to go, not having any security, feeling useless, and not ever knowing if or when he would have any food to fill the hunger in his belly."

After experiencing homelessness about five months, opportunities opened up for Ron. He ended up in the Los Angeles area with a very good job as Director of Marketing. He then rose to be Executive Vice President of Lite Source Inc. working for an understanding employer.

He was soon hooked again on helping the "least of our brethren," the homeless of Los Angeles. He formed the East San Gabriel Valley Coalition for the Homeless, Incorporated (ESGVCH) that began in September 8, 1994. He worked with thirty churches to operate a Winter Shelter, Emergency Assistance Center, and four transitional homes. He hired two full-time employees plus twelve seasonal employees. During the Winter Shelter program they had six hundred homeless person registered in the program. When he left, the ESGVCH was running on a budget of $127,000.00 a year after it had begun with $10-$50 in donations from local churches just a few years earlier.

Ron met his second wife, Doris at a New Years Eve party. While dating, she mentioned that she was going to deliver food to a homeless shelter for families with children. He asked if he could go along. The journey that had started at his mother's knee years ago, then living with "street people" who were experiencing homelessness, now paid off.

Rev. Dr. Hillary Chrisley of St. Matthews UMC, the same church that his future wife attended, was also involved. Hillary became Chairperson of an organization of associate pastors who helped to support the family homeless shelter, "Jobs Shelter," under the direction of Lutheran Social Services. Ron now had a good job that afforded him more resources than he needed.

Some monthly meetings were attended by only Hillary and Ron, and the organization was down to a very few members. Then in 1994 The Lutheran Social Services pulled up stakes in the East San Gabriel Valley and left the area. The closing of the Emergency Assistance Center left the area without either the Winter Shelter program or Jobs Shelter, the shelter for families. This part of the county now had almost no services for the homeless.

In late 1994 a group of six to eight persons with no money, but with great faith, got together. With the backing of the congregation of St. Matthews UMC and other churches they became incorporated into the East San Gabriel Valley Coalition For The Homeless. They also used money borrowed from Doris and Ron's checking account,

The ESGVCH now provides an Emergency Assistance Service Center that is open all year long. They also host the Winter Shelter Program open December through March. Each participating church hosts the winter shelter for two weeks, and then it revolves to another church. They also have a Transitional Home, Jobs II project, which houses two families who have become homeless and need a re-start in life. This coalition of churches, with over thirty churches participating in some manner, has provided safe havens for those less fortunate. Recently they registered well over four hundred persons, averaging one hundred and twenty per night, which included a significant increase in the number of families.

The spark, the fire, the enthusiasm generated from St. Matthews UMC made all of this possible. However through "burn out" and space limitations, the participation of Methodist churches in the Winter Shelter Program dropped to just one. St. Matthews hosted the shelter while a very few others supplied food. Ron finally resigned from the Presidency and the Board of Directors so that he could get back to working with people.

In September 2005, Ron and his wife moved to El Dorado County. He discovered the homeless citizens of the county and felt the need to do something for those who were abandoned by their local government. He first started working with United Outreach as a volunteer providing overnight support for the winter shelter held at the Seventh Day Adventist Church in Camino. That's where I met him.

From there he organized "Job's Shelters of the Sierra," (JSS) a non-profit corporation. It provides two vans filled with supplies that are manned by homeless citizens of El Dorado County. They visit the encampments and gathering places of homeless persons and pass out the necessities that they need to live in tents. Toilet paper, socks, candles, warm and dry clothing, books to read, as well as hygiene supplies are found in the supply vans which are seen in the encampments six days a week.

It is estimated that with this supply distribution, the vans give out 78 rolls of toilet paper and 136 pairs of socks each week. In addition, JSS is supplying the necessities of living in a tent in the woods. JSS has provided forty-nine tents and sleeping bags this season to every homeless person who finds himself in need. In the fall, heavy jackets and blankets are in high demand, and 250 of each of these items have been given out. Tarps, rope, batteries, clean underwear, pants, shirts, sweaters, hats, gloves, portable shower, shoes, boots, rain gear are all needed. Those demands are met by volunteer donations from churches, organizations and individuals as well as special purchases made by JSS.

Working with United Outreach, the JSS group of productive homeless persons organized, supplied, and managed one building called the "Supply Closet" at Grace Place at Perks Court. JSS organized a coalition consisting of United Outreach, JSS and Only Kindness and invited a food provider to join the coalition. Together they hoped to operate a shower and laundry

facility needed by the homeless community to counter the health issues that plague them.

Ron teaches adult Sunday school classes and Bible studies specializing in the first three hundred years of Christianity. He has been translating from Greek manuscripts some of the many first Christian writings about Jesus and His teachings. Bible translation has always been an interest to him, so with his collection of translations, he has forged ahead with "what did they say back then?" Bible studies, using the early manuscripts and the newer versions of the Bible are his passion. This has been his most enjoyable teaching. Teenagers are a "trip," and teaching them puts life in prospective.

In this process, Ron completed a course as a Lay Speaker. Being a church delegate to the Annual Conference allows him to expand his information and commitment to the Methodist ideas brought by John Wesley's statement. "Think and let think." Methodism allows him to examine history and question the changes in Christian thought throughout the ages.

He has tried hard to follow Matthew 25:40:

"I tell you the truth, whatever you did for one of the least my brothers, you did for me."

Our friendship and mutual respect has expanded over the years, and we work together today to build a homeless shelter here in El Dorado County. His friendship and support has been invaluable to me since 2006.

Ron Sachs

Doris Sachs

Ron Sachs

Ron Sachs With Homeless Friends

CHAPTER FOUR

Homeless Designations

It is a common belief that there are two distinct groups of homeless people, the "transitional" and the "chronic." Basically the difference between the two lies in their attitude toward being homeless and how long they have been living on the street. Of course, all designations like this are over-simplifications, and many homeless people transition back and forth between the two. However, let's take a look at the difference, and how it affects the way we view and treat them.

The transitional homeless are those men and women who, typically, just lost their job and home, whose spouse has deserted them, who have just returned from combat or whose parents just kicked them out of the house. This latter group is made up of mostly of teen-age foster kids. They are all usually looking for work and a place to stay that will take them off the streets, and they have, by definition, been homeless for less than a year. A few of this group have addictions, and most are basically able to care for themselves.

Our experience with transitional homeless is that they need only a boost up, a temporary helping hand and move them in the mainstream of society in short order. Many have addiction issues, and some have mental problems, which often are the causes for them becoming homeless. This is the group that most communities are more willing to help.

The chronic homeless, on the other hand, are those who have been homeless for more than a year and generally have a negative attitude toward getting out of the homeless life style. Many have addictions and/or mental disorders. This is the group that most people in the community refuse to help for reasons that are pretty obvious. Few of us can understand their attitudes, and our culture cannot accept why this group wants to stay where it

is. This is an example of society forcing its own policies and set of beliefs on other people who typically will not accept them.

I have talked to many members of the "chronic" group over the years, and their stories tend to be very similar. "I used to try to find a job and work my way out but was usually rejected, and I now have no desire to get back into society and prefer to live with my brothers and sisters here on the street." When I first met this group I was surprised that someone would not want to get out of homelessness. Lately I have come to believe that they are not being truthful about their feelings about being homeless.

This illustrates several important facts about the chronically homeless. First, they have developed a lifestyle that is familiar to them. They know how to stay safe, panhandle for the little money they need and avoid rejection every time they venture out into society. I am not a psychologist, but I have seen this attitude in many aspects of modern living. The fact is that when a person is unable to attain a certain goal in life, he or she finally says, "Oh I never really wanted to achieve that goal all along. I am happy with where I am." This re-occurring theme illustrates the human need not to be rejected and "lose" every time they try.

We have a chronically homeless man here in Placerville who can be seen every day near the entrance to the McDonalds fast food restaurant on Broadway. He is a local fixture in town and always stands on the sidewalk (shirtless in good weather) near the entrance driveway. He never says anything to people walking along the street or driving up in cars. He just stares at them without smiling. Many people, thinking he is starving, will hand him a bill. He thanks them, stuffs the bill in his pocket and turns to look at the next person.

There is an anti-panhandling law in effect in town, but he is not technically panhandling because he does not talk to anyone or ask directly for money. He drives the police crazy because what he is doing is perfectly legal, so they can't arrest him. When you talk to this man you discover that he is well educated and speaks several languages. A homeless friend of mine once told me when he asked this man why he remained homeless; the answer was, "Where else could I make $100 a day?"

The distinction outlined here seems to be important to those people and organizations that are supporting the homeless. We have always been asked, "Well, you are not providing help to the chronic homeless are you?" Normal middle class citizens might be able to justify to themselves that the "deserving poor" are helped. It is another matter for those who say they are satisfied with their homeless life style if, in fact, they are.

This brings up the question of why there is a morally stronger case to be made to help the one group of homeless and not the other. Don't they both need a roof over their heads and food to put in their stomachs? Many otherwise helpful people have to put their own assumptions and lifestyles into the equation before they can commit to helping.

In my experience, the chronic tend to need more help with mental issues and substance abuse. It is somewhat easier to help the transitional homeless. The counties usually stand ready to provide mental and other programs that are typically already on tap for their "normal" residence. Unfortunately, few seem to be ready to provide a shelter for any of the homeless.

I think that substance abuse is the one issue that turns off the community more than any other. Certainly there are many homeless men and women who drink too much alcohol or are hooked on one drug or another. People ask me, "Does alcoholism cause homelessness or does homelessness cause alcoholism?" I am sure that there are some of both. It would seem at first that it doesn't matter, but the way you deal with causes is based to some degree on their addictions and how they got into them. More about that will be coming up later.

Volunteers at Lumsden Park

CHAPTER FIVE

United Outreach

After a couple of months of feeding the homeless at the Camino Church, Raj asked me one day if I would like to join the Board ofDirectors of United Outreach. Shirley and I were becoming used to spending one or more nights a month at the church visiting with the homeless and agreed that I could be useful on the board, so I accepted. A couple of months later, Raj came to me and said, "Art, I'm leaving the area for another job and wonder if you would take over my spot as president of United Outreach?" I was surprised but agreed to accept the offer.

Our first task was to decide what to do about our twice-a-week shelter at the church. Winter was coming and two nights a week were not enough to keep the homeless men and women alive when it snowed. It was obvious that there were not enough volunteers available to do the job on an expanded basis. We would have to hire a professional to supervise the shelter but as we had no funds to pay anyone, I went to the county Board of Supervisors for help.

Fortunately, this was before the national economic bubble burst, so I asked the county to help us financially in operating the shelter until April of the following year. The Board of Supervisors was generous and gave us enough funding to keep the church shelter open during the winter. As I recall, it was the first and last time that we received any economic help from a government agency.

We hired a professional woman to oversee operations and supervise our volunteers. The church gym was now open five nights a week and closed on two, so that the congregation would have access to its gym twice a week.

Anyone who was homeless was welcome to spend the nights with us as long as they behaved in the shelter. Consequently, some of the people coming in were in various stages of drunkenness when they walked through the front door. With some exceptions, this was not a big problem, because most of our homeless who had had too much to drink headed straight for their beds and immediately fell sound asleep for the night. The church provided room dividers, mattresses, pillows and blankets for the homeless. Volunteers from area churches provided hot meals, snacks and beverages for their evening enjoyment.

Several ladies in Federated Church purchased a portable shower trailer from the state fire protection agency and had it delivered to the church to be used by the homeless. Every night, they lined up to get their warm showers. Of course, the church had a significant increase in its water bill during this period.

During that winter, a very sad event took place in Placerville. Before the Camino Church opened up as a shelter, many of the local homeless had set up tents on the hillside behind Lumsden Park. Over the months of living in their tents, the homeless typically accumulated some personal belongings, all of which were stored in their tents that were not lockable. Since the possibility of theft was very high, many homeless were reluctant to leave their tents for the night and sleep in the warm church. It was a tough decision for many to make.

One night in February, the temperature fell to a low in the teens. One woman apparently in her forties had too much to drink one afternoon and passed out causing her to miss the bus that would have taken her to the church. Whether she intentionally decided to stay in her tent that night or inadvertently missed the bus will never be known. The next morning she was found frozen to death in her sleeping bag.

Many men and women who suddenly became homeless that winter had had no experience living in tents and sleeping on the ground. They had to be trained quickly in how to survive living in the elements.

One day the nurse in our church called me to say that a young women was being evicted from her apartment the next day and asked if there were anything we could do to help her. She had never slept in a tent and had no idea how to survive out in the open. My wife, a friend and I went to Big 5 and K-mart to buy a tent, sleeping bag and other needed items and then stopped by the homeless camp at Lumsden Park.

I gathered together all the homeless living there and told them that I was bringing in a woman the next day who had no idea how to survive in a tent. I said that her survival was their responsibility and would hold them personally accountable if anything happened to her. The next morning my wife and I picked her up, drove her to the park and told the dozen or so men standing around, "Okay, here she is. I'll be back tomorrow morning and she'd better be alive." They all nodded, escorted her out of the park and up unto the hillside behind.

The next morning I drove into the park and saw a big group of homeless men and women sitting around a table on benches talking. I walked up to see our new homeless lady sitting in the center of the group talking and gesturing and basking in everyone's attention. One of the homeless guys turned to me and said, "Well, as you can see Art, she survived." They had leveled out a clearing in the forest, set up her tent, blew up her air mattress, spread out her sleeping bag and pillow and lectured her on how to survive in the wilderness. She turned out to be the hit of the camp for the several weeks she stayed there.

When the Seventh Day Adventist shelter closed late that spring, United Outreach concentrated on finding a new site for

a homeless shelter but first had to square away an important issue with the Camino Church.

Pastor Klatt, who was also a member of our board, told us one day that the homeless group that had been spending the winter nights at the church had badly damaged the gym floor. It is a basketball court, and the floor was constructed of finished hard wood that was highly polished. Many homeless men wore big boots as they walked on a floor that was intended to support tennis shoes only. The resulting damage was severe.

I told Pastor Klatt to get the floor repaired and United Outreach would pay the cost. A few weeks later he presented a bill for several hundred dollars and I wrote him a check for the full amount. It took a big bite out of our resources, but I would not let his generous church foot the bill for damage caused by our homeless population.

When the homeless men and women were turned out of the church and returned to their tents above Lumsden Park, I struck out on a search for a location for a permanent homeless shelter.

CHAPTER SIX

Don R.

Don Rake

D on's Journey to Hangtown Haven began when he started working in his early twenties for a large company for a few years. It didn't take long for him to decide that he wanted to do more than come up with ways to save company profits and value of its stock. He was young, idealistic, and wanted to make a difference.

He decided to go back to school and major in biology. At the time he wanted to get an advanced degree in marine sciences and become the next Jacques Cousteau. But by the time he was finishing his undergraduate education divorce loomed and reality settled in. He needed to go to work to pay child support.

A bachelor's degree in biology isn't worth much; one can get a low-paying and boring job in a lab, but that's about it. Don managed to get a position with the State of California in a totally non-scientific job at the State's Personnel Board. He enjoyed the work and stayed there for about three years before an opportunity came up to transfer to the Air Resources Board, California's air pollution agency. At age 32, he was finally working at a place where he could use his science education and contribute to making the world a better place. After 27 years at

the ARB, Don retired at age 59. The ARB was an outstanding but stressful place to work, and he was burned out.

Don and his wife decided to move somewhere with more natural beauty than the Sacramento Valley and settled in Placerville, California, in the Sierra foothills. Being retired and having plenty of spare time, he looked for volunteer opportunities that would serve the disadvantaged in the area. He volunteered at the El Dorado County Food Bank for a few months but that was primarily office work and he wanted something more hands-on. Don then went to the Community Resource Center, a local non-profit that seeks to link the disadvantaged community with services to help them improve their lives. Because of the variety and number of clients at CRC, there was rarely a dull moment as homeless men and women came in every day.

During his tenure at CRC, Hangtown Haven, a local homeless shelter had opened. It was established as a self-governing camp for the homeless. A community council consisting of the homeless would run the day-to-day operation of the camp, and, very importantly, would enforce the very strict rules that residents could not violate without being expelled from the camp.

During the early days of the camp there was a bit of a Wild West atmosphere that made Don wonder if it could be viable for the long-term. After a few months of operation, the Hangtown Haven, Inc. Board of Directors decided that the camp needed a volunteer component to provide a more stable environment for the residents. Don's experience at CRC told him that this approach made sense and was doable. Many of the homeless just needed a little positive reinforcement from someone who had been successful in life to encourage them to improve their situation. He was very impressed with what he saw at Hangtown Haven. The influx of outside volunteers would prove to stabilize the camp and have a calming effect on its atmosphere.

Don offered to be the volunteer coordinator, and eventually I asked him also to be Director of Operations of Hangtown Haven after Ron Sachs resigned. Don and I have always had a great respect for one another, and I think Don had trouble saying no to my request. As volunteer coordinator, he had the responsibility of recruiting and organizing new volunteers. It worked well as some of the new volunteers also recruited people they knew. Don recruited mainly by getting publicity in the local press, contacting churches and service organizations, and talking to just about anyone who expressed interest. Experienced volunteers trained new volunteers. We were all very pleased with the quality of volunteers we were able to recruit. This was a wonderful group of very committed people that we are now proud to call good friends. Working together in an environment like Hangtown Haven and sharing in the successes we made there resulted in strong long-term friendships.

After a few months and a couple of minor missteps, Hangtown Haven became very successful. We had begun developing the expertise and contacts to align the residents of Hangtown Haven with services and employment opportunities. A couple of examples: Fred (not his real name) came into the camp from a seriously bad living environment. Several meth users lived in the same house, and Fred was a diabetic as well as a serious alcoholic and drug addict. He came into Hangtown Haven a total mess. Some of the volunteers set Fred up with Alcoholics Anonymous and drug therapy groups. Don also taught him how to buy and prepare healthy food to help mitigate his diabetes problems. He had not been taking his insulin regularly and Don got him onto a schedule. Fred's life improved rapidly, and he was very grateful for all efforts on his behalf.

"Betty" was pregnant and camping illegally without proper medical attention or prenatal care appeared at the camp. She was given a tent and a safe place to stay at Hangtown Haven.

She was very nervous about everyone and everything. One of the female volunteers took Betty under her wing, gained Betty's trust, and set Betty up with a local agency to get proper prenatal care.

Unfortunately, just as we were just starting to develop a lot of success stories, our temporary use permit expired in November of 2013, and the City of Placerville refused to extend it. Even though we operated at no cost to the City or County, politics got in the way and, just like that, we were shut down. We had to get everyone and everything off the property in just two weeks. While this was an emotional blow to Don personally, it was a catastrophe for the residents. Besides losing the support provided by the Hangtown Haven organization, the residents had to find somewhere else to live or maybe just exist. We were just getting into the beginning of winter weather and the only alternative available to most of the residents was the winter nomadic shelter program, which is very limited in what it can provide.

CHAPTER SEVEN

Homeless Grant

In the late spring of 2007, we heard that the State of California was offering grants to counties to build and operate homeless shelters in their communities. El Dorado County asked United Outreach to find a piece of property that would be appropriates for a homeless shelter, then design a building on it and develop an operational system that would guarantee a permanently successful shelter for the homeless. Since United Outreach was the only non-profit corporation in the county that had operated its own successful nighttime shelter program, we were a natural choice to be a partner with the county. I was also instructed to write a proposal to the county with associated costs and designs when I found the property. They would then use my proposal to go to the state requesting the grant. As I recall, the grant amounted to about $1.5 million.

United Outreach had by this time expanded its board of directors to six people and we were raising money from the community based on our success the previous year. My high school sweetheart in Walnut Creek, who was a millionaire owner of an insurance firm, sent me a check for $10,000 to help our cause. We were flying high as I searched the county for a building or a property that could be used for a homeless shelter. To begin the search, I employed the help of a realtor at Coldwell Banker who gave me addresses and accompanied me as we toured the county.

I typically drove out several times a week searching for a property that would fit the state and county requirements for a shelter able to house maybe fifty men and women. For only $1.5 million, an existing building would need to be a part of the property.

It took a while, but I eventually found a piece of property in Camino on Pony Express Trail (old highway 50). It had a nice building on it that was large enough and could be used with a little modification to house forty to fifty homeless people in barracks style living. I went to work on my drafting table to create a design that expanded on the existing building.

It was about this time that I met a man who would become, and still is, a very good friend. His name is Peter Wolfe, a licensed architect practicing here in town. I went into his office on Broadway one day to ask him to help me work out the legal and design requirements for a building that would sleep fifty people. I discovered that he was a retired Coast Guard officer, and so we shared sea stories on our first meeting and got little done on the design of our homeless shelter! Peter soon made a beautiful rendering of the building as we would design it, and I put together an operational plan to present to the county. Peter was, and still is devoted to helping the homeless, and we still hope to build a homeless shelter together some day.

The property had been leased to the Lutheran Church, but the congregation was moving to a new location, so the property was for lease. The owner, a very nice young man whose name I have lost, was very excited about using his building as a homeless shelter. He had lived in the neighborhood for most of his life and assured me that he could convince his neighbors that having a homeless shelter in their neighborhood would be no problem. I thought he was being overly optimistic but did nothing to discourage his optimism.

This may be a good time to discuss an important side issue, which is that of homeowners' lack of enthusiasm for having a homeless shelter in their community. It is probably obvious to people reading this story that many people view having homeless living nearby as a sure sign that home values will deteriorate when the word gets out. However, we had not experienced this

problem at our Adventist Church shelter located just down the road. However, it is not easy to predict with any accuracy how a neighboring community will respond to having a homeless shelter in its neighborhood.

This situation is not unlike the one which occurred during the 1950's and 60's when real estate agents used scare tactics to warn people that, "Blacks were moving into the neighborhood, so you'd better put your home on the market before your home value drops any more." Possibly home values did drop when owners thought that "homeless" were coming in, but I think that any drop was caused more by scare tactics used by some fanatics.

In California, homeless shelters can only be built in designated zones, usually "commercial". There are normally few homes in these zones because homes are normally built in "single family dwelling" zones, not commercial. There is no over arching way to handle this issue of which I am aware, but we were prepared to move into our new home in Camino and let the chips fall where they might. All we needed was the county's support and the state grant approval.

CHAPTER EIGHT

Working With County Employees

Everything was going well until I reported to the county that we had found a building in Camino. I was met with cold stares rather than the enthusiasm I was expecting. The county leaders did not tell me "no;" they just turned me over to a man who was to become my good friend, Mike Applegarth, a senior administrative analyst for El Dorado County. He had obviously been assigned to swing me in the direction the county wanted.

As we were driving around one day, Mike asked me, "Art, would you be interested in looking at a piece of property that could be used for a homeless shelter other than the one you've identified in Camino?"

'Sure. Why not?"

It was obvious to me that Mike was giving me an important message that he did not want to deliver directly. It didn't matter to me what property we used as long as we could put homeless on it. Mike continued. "This property is owned by the county and would therefore cost nothing. It has three buildings already on it and is ready to go."

I was getting more excited as he drove me onto Missouri Flat Road. He turned south and then immediately turned left onto Perks Court. It curled back toward the freeway and then ran along it as it dropped down toward Weber Creek. We shortly came to the property, and, Mike pulled up in front of a building.

As we got out of the car, I said something like, "It's a beautiful piece of property with two homes and one barn on it. It looks great but could it use more buildings. There are two homes and one barn on it and is flat and relatively secluded." However,

there was a vital piece of information that Mike soon filled me in on.

"This property has one problem for a homeless shelter, Art. It is zoned residential, not commercial. As you know, that means that we can sleep only six unrelated people in these buildings."

"Okay, so we get the zoning changed. How big a deal is that? The two lots next to this one are zoned commercial. Why is this one residential?"

"Changing zoning is not impossible, but it can be extremely difficult. However, we can cross that bridge later. Right now my question is do you think we could use these buildings for a homeless shelter?" Mike asked.

"Yes, absolutely," I replied after looking around a bit.

The main building was a three-bedroom two-bath home with a good-sized living room. The county engineering department was using it as a field office, and the field engineer stationed there wasn't too happy about seeing me. He had apparently been told that he was about to lose his office.

After a complete tour, Mike said to me, "The County would prefer that you use this property, Art, rather than the one in Camino." I could smell politics in the air. "If we get that state grant, maybe we could get the board to agree to a zoning change, and you could build a good sized shelter on it." I nodded skeptically.

"Okay, I'll get to work on a proposal and design that would include an additional building here and try to get approval." This was to be my second (or third) design of a homeless shelter, but if this is what the county wanted, then so be it. I went to work at my drafting table.

Several weeks before, the El Dorado County Irrigation District had offered to give United Outreach a three bedroom

pre-manufactured home that they no longer needed it if we would pay to move it. When I saw the property on Perks Court, it occurred to me that there was room at the rear of the property for this home, so I invited Montgomery Contractors in Sacramento to come up and give me a price to move the home from the EID station just east of Pollock Pines to the property on Perks Court. The owner, Steve Montgomery gave me a price of $10,000 so I went to work raising it.

My plan was to build a multi-story shelter in the front (north) side of the property and then use the existing home and the new EID home to house families. When its zoning was changed to commercial, or when we were able to get a Special Use Permit, there would be no restriction on the number of people we could sleep there.

We soon raised sufficient funds to move the EID building and contracted for its move. It went smoothly and we now had four buildings on the property. However the zoning allowed us to sleep only six homeless people in the front building.

I now began to prepare a proposal for the state grant based on building a homeless shelter on the county's property on Perks Court. I once again read through the grant outline given to the county by the state. Only this time I saw something that I had overlooked before. I saw for the first time in the grant's fine print a requirement that I paraphrase here:

"The county that receives this grant will guarantee to the state that, within five years, it will raise the equivalent amount of money that is in this grant locally and will use it to continue this project beyond the five years. If the county is not able to raise the amount within the five years, the county agrees to return the grant to the state in full."

I was shocked both to have missed this requirement the first time around as well as the shortsighted requirement by the

state. I immediately called Mike and told him about it. He said he would get back to me. He later called back to say that the County Board of Supervisors would take up the issue at their next meeting the following week. There was no doubt in my mind that the board would refuse to pursue the grant and the homeless would be without a shelter again.

In an attempt to head off the county's complete rejection of the plan to help the homeless, I composed a letter to the Board of Directors on Oct 4, 2008 that I hoped they would read before their next meeting. The letter is reproduced at the end of this chapter, but in essence it proposed to the board that, if they rejected the grant because of this requirement, United Outreach would support this decision. In lieu of this grant we would propose that the county lease to United Outreach the Perks Court property for a dollar a year and let us run a homeless shelter in the existing building that would be limited to six homeless women and children at a time. This was not what I had hoped for, but it seemed that it was all we could get. It was my plan that once we got the property, we could petition the board to change its zoning from residential to commercial and we could build a shelter on it.

In the meantime, the Board of Supervisors had asked me if I would guarantee that United Outreach could raise $1.5 million in gifts to match the state grant within the time frame as the grant proposal requires. I, of course, said that we would do all we could to raise that amount but certainly couldn't guarantee success.

I was being honest but it was not what the board wanted to hear, so at the next board meeting they brought up the issue. I think that I testified to the effect that it would be difficult for our community to raise that much money and it might fall back on the county to pay it out of tax revenue. They did not like this and voted to reject the grant as I had suspected that they would.

Members of The October 5, 2008
El Dorado County
Board of Supervisors

Dear Members of The Board:

As you know, United Outreach is working with the county to provide a homeless shelter and recovery program here in El Dorado County. The success of this program is based on the receipt of a grant from the state, which, we understand, will soon be presented to the Board of Supervisors for approval. We have been working with county agencies to develop a budget, select a site and plan a recovery program to be submitted for your consideration so that you accept the state's grant with confidence.

In recent conversations with county agencies, we have learned that the state grant comes to the county with certain requirements that are harsh in the extreme. The state apparently requires that United Outreach guarantee that it will continue to receive sufficient funds to operate successfully for a five-year period beyond the end of the three-year grant. This stipulation requires that we prove that these funding sources will be available at least eight years into the future. This requirement cannot be met.

United Outreach is a volunteer, non-profit organization dedicated to the support of homeless people in the county and is totally dependent for its survival on the generosity of individuals, churches, civic-minded organizations and government jurisdictions. It is impossible to guarantee the existence or continuation of this support for eight years. Most knowledgeable indicators show a continuing drop in the economy in our community, with an unknown date for a turn-around and a return to pre-recession financial conditions.

It is our understanding that the results of potential financial failure of the homeless shelter during the next eight years would result in the county paying back the $1.47 mil grant from its tax revenue. In addition, financial failure would also result in no state grants being awarded to the county for many years to come. We cannot, in good conscience, put our county in this position. Because we our unable to guarantee that United Outreach can maintain a continuing stream of income during that period, we respectfully request that we no longer be considered as a participant in the state grant contract.

United Outreach will continue to search for financial support from the private sector in hopes of providing a shelter and recovery program for the homeless of our county. We thank the county and its agencies for their help, support and encouragement during the three years of our existence.

Sincerely,

Art Edwards, President,

United Outreach

Let me back up a bit. Supervisor Jack Sweeney and I had been meeting privately for several weeks prior to the board meeting. I had drawn up a design of the building in Camino and presented it to him before we had heard about Perks Court. He seemed to like the idea but made one very significant remark during our meeting:

"I will do whatever I can to help homeless people who are trying to get out of homelessness, but I will do nothing to help the chronic homeless who intend to spend their entire lives in that situation." Here is that old, "chronic verses transitional" argument again.

I respected Jack's position and still consider him to be a good friend although I didn't always agree with his position. He has now retired but at least he was willing to go out on a limb and lease a piece of county property to us on which we could sleep six homeless people. In this county that was a brave gesture in this county considering the opposition. When I asked him about his decision later he said, "I've been elected supervisor for so many years that no one even bothers to run against me any more. I don't really care what people think. I'm only going to do what's right." My hat still goes off to you Jack.

Seeing that the state's grant offer was not viable, I made the following counter proposal to the board.

PRESENTATION TO THE BOARD OF DIRECTORS
8-25-09
BY: ART EDWARDS

1. ## INTRODUCTION

     A. $1.47 mil. Grant decision

     B. Perks Court is usable

2. ## SUMMARY OF LETTER

     A. Requirement to return $1.47 mil if default

     B. We cannot guarantee raising that amount of money

     C. Default means unable to raise $24,000 per month

     D. It's the county's decision to accept or reject the grant

     E. We will support you if you decide to reject the grant

3. ## UNITED OUTREACH WOULD LIKE TO MAKE AN ALTERNATE PROPOSAL

     A. If grant is rejected, lease perks court to us for $1 a year for 20 years

     B. Then let us develop the property and homeless program

     C. We will design and build a homeless facility

     D. We have been unable to raise much money because we have no property

     E. We will start small. It will take time. Santa Cruz example

F. Main advantage would be that there would be no state looking over our shoulders

4. **HAVE BROKEN THE PROJECT INTO SEVEN PHASES FOR CLARITY**

   A. Prepare the property, start the special use permit process.

   B. Six homeless people in existing home

   C. Deliver a third building from EID

   D. Build and install utilities

   E. Design the final lot and building configuration

   F. When the SUP is complete, buy and install additional buildings

   G. Build a common building

5. **WE HAVE NO FUNDS NOW**

   A. We will build as money becomes available

   B. P. It will take homeless off the streets of Placerville

6. **LOCATION IS PERFECT**

   A. EDC, community health center is close

   B. Restaurants are close by

   C. Bus service is close

   D. Food bank is near

   E. KMART is close

7. **NEAREST NEIGHBOR IS ¼ MILE AWAY**

   A. Invisible from the freeway

8. **ZONING IS NOT APPROPRIATE, WILL NEED A SPECIAL USE PERMIT (SUP)**

9. **ROAD WORK**

A. Design looks like road will not take up too much of the property.

B. Whatever is required of the county or contractor, we will do. Flexible!

C. We assume that the county will move the road to accommodate the three properties that it owns.

10. WINTER IS COMING

A. People are living in forests and parks, increasing fire danger in the county

B. United Outreach is providing food and rooms in motels

C. That money will soon run out

11. SUMMARY

We hope that the county will work with United Outreach to provide the beginnings of a facility for the homeless and allow us to develop its Perks Court property into a first class homeless facility.

The board has never responded to my proposal so I made another suggestion:

PROPOSAL FOR PERKS COURT TRANSITIONAL HOUSING CENTER

This was a proposal I wrote to the Board of Supervisors that would change its zoning from "Residential" to "Commercial" so that we could house more than six homeless residents on the Perks Court property.

Rather than the county accepting the state homeless grant of $1.47 million United Outreach proposes the following alternative:

Our proposal is that the county rejects the state grant and, instead, leases the three acre perks Court property to United Outreach for twenty years for a dollar per year, effective immediately. This will allow United Outreach to begin raising money to build a transitional homeless center on the property without the state schedule and budget requirements hanging over the county's head. With private donations, corporate gifts and government grants, United Outreach will immediately begin the design and construction of a modern homeless center on the site at no cost to the county. As funds become available, the following will be accomplished:

1. With the county's help, the zoning on the property will be changed from "Residential" to "Commercial", and all engineering design will be accomplished.

2. The west edge of the property will be cut back approximately eight feet and a six-foot retaining wall will be built.

3. The septic system will be enlarged.

4. Water and power will be expanded.

5. The EID building will be brought in and installed along the east side of the property.

6. The portable shower and laundry trailer will be brought in and installed.

7. The existing buildings will be cleaned, modified as necessary and made ready to house homeless families.

8. Port-a-potties will be installed.

9. Shelter will be designed for northwest segment.

10. A shelter will be built.

Leasing Perks Court to United Outreach has several advantages:

- It costs the county nothing except appropriate support from staff.

- Neither the county nor United Outreach is constrained by state mandated schedules.

- The site will be expanded as funds become available.

- Having a site simplifies the fund raising process for United Outreach and the county.

- The site will be available for county road engineers if needed for the construction of Missouri Flat interchange.

- The county will be doing something positive for the homeless.

Unfortunately for the homeless, the board took no action on this proposal either and the property remains zoned "Residential" to this day and six homeless people moved in to the home. The EID building remains unoccupied.

Perks Court Buildings

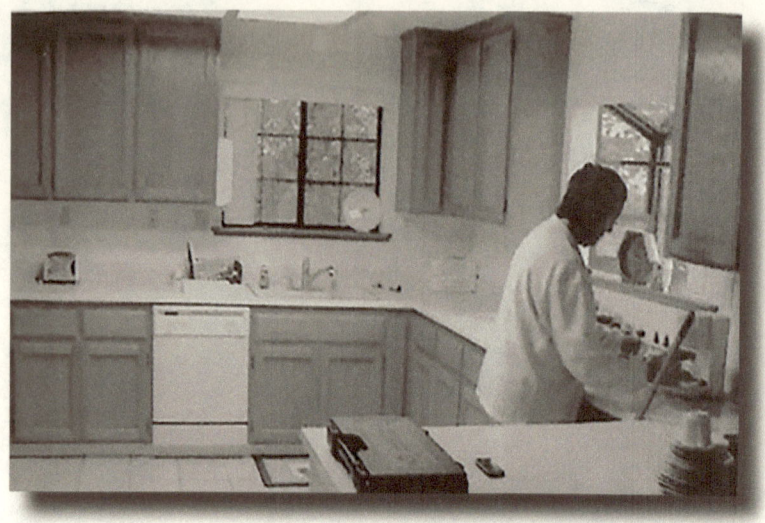

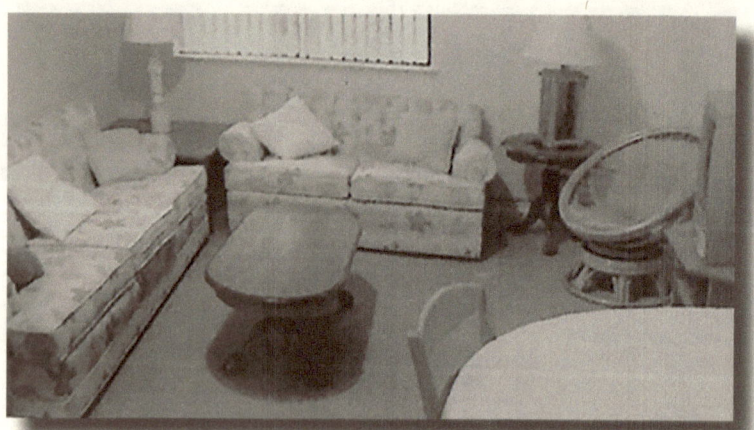

Perks Court

CHAPTER NINE

Ken G.

Ken Green

K en is the second oldest of 4 kids and is the only boy in the family. He always said that the responsible part of his life started at about twelve years old. He remembers really wanting a skateboard. His parents told him that, "If you want something bad enough you'll work for it, and if you work for it we'll help you." Ken mowed lawns and did yard work all summer long and saved up enough money to buy the best skateboard around. His mom said that he was responsible and that she was proud of him. It was the first time in his life that he realized that he had made his mom proud.

He was not a good student in school. The summer of his thirteenth year, his mom and step-dad divorced and his stepdad left the family. Ken felt like it was his job to step up and care for the family. He worked all summer long to buy a single steer so that the family could have a freezer full of meat. Once again his mom was proud of him, but that was probably the last time that he remembers of his mom saying she was proud of him for many years.

When he was sixteen he started his own painting business when he was 16 and dropped out of school. With business came more responsibility, and more money led to addictions. Between

ages sixteen to twenty four he basically worked for drugs and alcohol. He lost his business at 25 and ended up in Nevada.

It was there that he started his first family with a wife and two children. He went to work in one of the casinos making a good salary. Unfortunately, his income led to the destruction of his family by giving him access to drugs and alcohol. He soon re-married as his income increased and still worked in the casinos in better jobs. He had four more children but hadn't learn from prior mistakes He lost custody of his four children and went to jail for the first time.

He became clean and sober for a short time, long enough to get his children back and, with his wife, moved to California. He got a job at a trailer park in Amador County, but soon started doing drugs again. This led to his wife taking their children and moving to Reno, so he moved to Reno to be near his family. Unfortunately, he was not clean and sober nor in the right frame of mind to help his wife and children. As a result, the two of them went to jail and lost permanent custody of their family. Ken has not seen them since 2005.

He eventually moved to Arizona and moved in with his mother. He was able to bring his kids to Arizona for a great Christmas with his mom and family. After his children returned to Nevada, he proceeded to get high over and over again. He lived in Arizona for about a year and was high the whole time. His mom finally decided that they should move back to Amador County. He stayed up for a week packing and then drove his mom back to Amador County. He unloaded the U-Haul at a storage facility and stayed with some friends. On our return trip, his friend drove the truck and he drove his mother in his car.

While driving along at sixty-five miles an hour, he fell asleep behind the wheel. The car drifted off of the road and ran under

the back of the car ahead and then off the road. When he lifted his mom out of the car she was limp and seemed lifeless. That was the first time he remembered God stepping into his life and taking charge. God was in control. Fortunately, the wreck took place right next to a fire department building. It only took a minute for the fire department get there and start helping his mom until a helicopter arrived in nine minutes.

The fireman in charge told his friend that he knew Ken was under the influence, but that he had enough to deal with and just to take Ken home. His mom spent three weeks in a coma and three months in rehabilitation in the hospital. For the next year Ken got heavier into drugs, couch surfing trying to stay stoned. He had had enough of life, and nothing seemed to be working, and things were just getting worse. His mom finally went back to Arizona, so that his older sister could care for her. The only good news about the accident was that, although she had been given six months to live, her COPD seemed to improve, and she is still alive today.

He was definitely below rock bottom, and being alone, he needed his family. He knew that his sister Kim was homeless in Placerville living in a tent. So on the morning of Nov. 4, 2011 he grabbed a duffle bag and stuffed it with all the clothes that would fit and walked uphill from Plymouth to Placerville. At the Placerville city limits, a person picked him up and gave him a ride to the Upper Room late in the afternoon. The only people willing to help with him no questions asked were the homeless people at the Upper Room. They showed him how to go to the shelters where he lived while searching for his sister.

It took sixteen days to find her, and he believes it was thanks to the prayers of Patricia at Green Valley Community Church that did the trick. While he was in the shelters he was introduced to the Community Resource Center on Upper Broadway in Placerville where he met some wonderful people. He hung out

with everybody for about two months and finally realized that he could live without drugs and actually could make something of himself. He was clean and sober and soon began to volunteer at the CRC and at the homeless shelters in the area. He did that until the night shelters ended, but continued to volunteer at the CRC until the shelter season started again. When the shelter season began he met wonderful people like Todd Parker, Rebecca Nylander, Larry Allum and Chris McClain.

At the end of the season Marie Cook the director of the CRC gave him a home for three months. It was at that time that I approached Ken about the idea of living in Hangtown Haven. He thought I was out of my mind, but thought, "What the heck, let's give it a try."

Ken moved into the Haven, took a leadership role and was soon elevated to second in command of the resident council. When Larry left for a job in Texas, Ken took over the council presidency and proved to be an outstanding leader until the shelter was closed by the city a few months later.

CHAPTER TEN

A Bad Mistake

I expanded the United Outreach board of directors by bringing on three new people, all women. Two of them had had experience in working with homeless so I thought it would be a good idea to broaden our prospective. It turns out that I made a fatal mistake, at least for me.

With help from several churches, mostly Faith Episcopal in Cameron Park, and Federated Church in Placerville, we made the home habitable and the EID building on the road for occupancy. Our board set up requirements for the homeless to live in the home, and I began to work on the county to approve the transition of the property to commercial, so that we could expand the number of homeless we could take in.

Everyone did a great job, and the home was soon ready to accept the six homeless women and children as residents. The board came up with several rules for living there that were not to my liking. For instance, they ruled that the residents could not spend the days in the home but had to be out looking for a job every day except on weekends. They also made the rule that no one could live in our facility for more than six months. I thought that both of these requirements were a bit excessive, but our new board members outvoted me.

I also made the garage into a perfect storage room for clothes, putting in hangers and shelves. It was my intention to give the space to Jobs Shelters of the Sierra (JSS) for their use. JSS was (and is) run by my old friend, Ron Sachs. He needed a space to store the clothes and other sundries his organization passes out to the homeless on the streets. Several times a week he and his volunteers can still be seen driving around in his SUV packed with clothes, toilet paper and other items needed by those who have no home. The alternative was to rent a storage locker somewhere for the clothes. United Outreach had no use for the building, so I thought that my board would be willing to use the building to help the homeless in this way. Wrong again!

The Author Supervising Operations

After several weeks I came to the conclusion that it was going to be impossible to convince the county that we should change the zoning so that we could build a facility to house more than six homeless people. There was apparently just too much political pressure in the county from people who wanted to do nothing more than house the six homeless women and children

now living on our beautiful Perks Court property. It was going to stay zoned residential. I was totally frustrated and, because of the county's attitude, my friend Peter resigned from our board in frustration. In addition to facing opposition from the county government, my board of directors disagreed with me on every issue. Something had to be done.

I made the critical decision to resign from United Outreach and search for another route to build a homeless shelter in the community. Unfortunately, when I quit, the United Outreach board voted to expel Ron Sachs and his JSS clothes storage closet although they had no other plans for the building. I assume this was a move to get back at me for not knuckling under to our new board. I was very disappointed but could see that all the United Outreach board wanted was to house the six women and children that the county allowed on the property and nothing more. I had bigger fish to fry.

It is interesting as a side note that in 2014 United Outreach decided to stop using the Perks Court house to provide a home for the homeless women and children who had been using it. After they left we inspected the building to see in what condition they had left the building. The interior was very clean, but we were shocked to discover that everything in the interior had been removed. It was completely empty! There was no furniture, beds, nor even kitchen plates and utensils. It had been stripped clean of the thousands of dollars in furniture donations made originally to make the home livable. I was unable to find out what had happened to it all. Apparently United Outreach had given it away and then folded up completely.

The lesson here is be sure you know whom you are inviting onto your board of directors.

I thought I did and then found out differently.

Architect Peter Wolfe at Work

Truck Delivering EID Building

Existing Building on Perks Court

EID Building Being Assembled

CHAPTER ELEVEN

Non-Producttive Years

The four years between 2010 and 2013 were non-productive in building a homeless shelter in El Dorado County. I searched for help from the county Board of Supervisors and eventually from the city of Placerville. Ron Sachs and I checked all the records for a county-owed property that was zoned commercial and would be appropriate on which to build a shelter. Nothing showed up, and nobody in power stepped up to offer assistance. I made speeches at the Rotary Club, Kiwanis, in churches; I tried to contact the Masons but they did not respond. I even wrote letters to the editor of the local newspaper. My reputation developed as I became somewhat notorious as an advocate for the homeless. I accomplished nothing except to make our community more aware of the homeless people around us. I was told that I also had angered some wealthy and politically powerful people in the community in the process.

Some authors who tell stories of conflict and endless confrontation use metaphors to describe what they are going through. "Rowing across an endless sea," "Searching for the light at the end of the tunnel," "Crossing a trackless desert," seem to be some favorites. I have searched for an appropriate metaphor to describe my attempt to build a shelter for the homeless in the county, but none that sounds appropriate have come to mind.

My efforts during this period were always unsuccessful. All I could do was to get up off the canvas and confront my opponents again before they beat me down again. Okay, so now I am using a boxing metaphor. I never learned to box, much to my dad's disappointment, but he and I always watched the Friday night fights on TV together as I tried to stay awake. The boxing metaphor does seem to be appropriate though in trying

to help the homeless. A number of friends have commented that I just don't know when I am licked.

I read a story in our local paper about the county appropriating $7 million to build a new animal shelter, and my anger rose. I naturally had to write a letter to the editor complaining that the county would spend $7 million on dogs and not one red cent on homeless. I ended up my letter by saying that I would like to spend my next life as a dog in El Dorado County.

I received no response except that someone told me that the $7 million was donated money not tax dollars,

However, this brings up a good point that should have been a lesson to me and to all of us. People think more of their dogs than they do of homeless human beings, including veterans! This last point is the most tragic. I have nothing against pets, but, after all, dogs are only dogs. We've seen homeless veterans who have just returned from Iraq, many with PTSD. There are still homeless men living on the streets who were in the Vietnam War. Where is the VFW, the American Legion? Where are the citizens who send young men and women off to fight foreign wars, and then refuse to provide a shelter for those who can't cope with society when they return?

Many well-off citizens I have talked to refuse to even accept the fact the homeless veterans are living amongst us, being arrested every day by our police and sheriff departments for sleeping on street corners or on private property. Why does this bother me so? I am a veteran of the Korean War, my dad was in World War II, my grandfather tried to enlist in the Spanish War (he was rejected because he had miner's consumption from which he died twenty years later) and I have two great grandfathers who were in the Union Army during the Civil War. It would bother me just as much if we were not a family of

veterans. It apparently does not bother the powerful citizens of our community who don't want to hear about it.

During this period, I joined the El Dorado Continuum of Care here in the county. Its original purpose was to help non-profits obtain federal and state grants and to train people to use the HMIS computer program. The purpose of the HMIS system is to give all non-profits a database so that when a homeless person checks in to our facility, we will have instant access to his complete medical and mental history in our community.

The CoC talked about finding grants and other financial aid for us. After several meetings with the group, I asked its leader, Scott Thurmond, if he thought that there was any possibility that we could get a grant from the government. His answer was honest and to the point, "No, I don't think so," he responded. I appreciated his honesty, but soon stopped going to the meetings. There was no point in continuing to attend meetings that would lead to a dead end. I like Scott. He is dedicated to helping the homeless and very knowledgeable about finding grants.

CHAPTER TWELVE

Lisa

W e first met Lisa about eight or nine years ago behind K-mart when Ron first began the Job's Shelters of the Sierra ministry. Lisa was the "mother hen" of one of about four communities of homeless people living in the Manzanita brush behind K-Mart. Lisa had set up a "palace" of sorts with her tents. She had her sleeping tent set up within a larger tent. She also had a smaller "storage" tent set up nearby. She was warm and dry even during the winter months. We were quite impressed with her whole layout.

She kept the others in her flock under her wing and under loose control. In the evenings they would sit around a campfire and trade stories, each having something to share. They all knew where the best place to panhandle and would discuss the rumors and gossip of the day.

The other groups camping nearby had their own group personalities; one was composed of alcoholics. They each lived in a combination of tent and tent parts, with empty bottles and containers covering the area. This group was mostly incoherent and all stoned by 1:00 PM. Another group was into making "meth" and used and distributed drugs for resale. They also had a "family" of all ages from a baby to adults many of whom were shoplifters, con artists, and did anything legal or illegal to survive.

Their site was located next to a county graveyard and was set up with multi tents to accommodate its various "family" members. JSS visited all of those sites Mondays, Wednesday, and Friday and it was one of the most interesting, rewarding, and heartfelt experiences of Ron's lifetime.

This all fell apart when one of Lisa's flock shot another member over a dispute about the need to return something that was being held as collateral for a loan that was not paid.

Lisa was a homemaker and her husband had a well-paying job as a pile-driving technician for a bridge construction company; they owned a home and had two teenage boys in school.

One morning the oldest boy went outside and suddenly saw his father dangling by the neck from a tree in a suicide attempt. The oldest son, who was present while Lisa was telling me this, made the comment, "He couldn't even do that right." Lisa heard her son yell, came out of the house, cut the rope, and her husband fell to the ground. An ambulance was called, but he died before getting to the hospital. There was some money in the house that she lived on, but soon the bills and the creditors came, and Lisa and her sons lost everything they had.

Although her husband made very good money, he gambled it all away. Eventually everything they owned was taken as security for money to pay the gambling debts.

Everything was gone! Lisa was forced to live on the streets, as she has no marketable skills. Her oldest son followed in her footsteps. Her younger son continued going to high school, "couch surfing" until he graduated. He joined the Army and got married in the last year or two. Lisa and her older son continued to live together on the streets and were reduced to doing whatever they needed to do to survive. She obtained a job with a non-profit firm here in El Dorado County, but pretty soon lost that job for multiple reasons. It is very difficult to keep a job when you are homeless.

During that time she found a place for herself and her older son, and she even acquired an automobile; sadly she couldn't get out of the culture of homelessness, and through her actions she lost it all.

Recently at age 48, Lisa died of liver failure probably caused by substance and alcohol abuse. This story plays out many times in El Dorado County and in every county in the United States. Lisa and her older son hated and condemned banks for taking away everything they had. She indicated to Ron at one time that she had checks and therefore thought that there was money in her account. Even though Lisa was smart, it appears that she didn't have the concept that you need money in the bank to write checks or make withdrawals. She lacked "living" skills that many of us take for granted.

Unfortunately, Lisa's story is a classic example of a family that is devastated by events that are beyond a mother's control. For some reason, many middle class people believe, or say they do, that homelessness is the result of some misbehavior of the people involved. She is a typical example of just the opposite. People are often the victim of circumstances that are far beyond their control. Some we saw at Hangtown Haven were able to cope with their extreme misfortune, and some are overwhelmed by it. Who are we to judge other people's ability to react to the misfortunes of life?

Lisa

CHAPTER THIRTEEN

Who Are We Trying To Help?

Earlier in chapter 4, I identified the two groups of homeless, the chronic and the transitional. Unfortunately, our public tends to lump all homeless into the first group and justify their refusal to help any homeless by saying, "Why should I help someone who only wants to live off of handouts and refuses to get a job and help himself?" It is best to ignore such stupid comments, but I can't always. Sometimes I to try to develop a logical reasoned argument that shows that most homeless want to get back into a job and a home just as you and I would. However this is an argument that tends to overlook the realities of the homeless community.

First of all, it is important that readers understand the difference between these two groups if you are trying to build and develop a homeless shelter in your community. Some non-profits just put a time limit on living in the facility. "You have six months to find a job or you are out," I have heard this argument more than once. It is wrong for several reasons:

- Getting a job depends as much on the economy as on personal skills.

- The homeless person probably needs job training most of all.

- Many women need child support to get a job.

- Many homeless view this rule as a negative that cause them worry every day.

- This rule automatically excludes chronic homeless from the shelter.

This brings us to the main question, "Do we want to help the chronic homeless in the first place?" This is an important early

decision that everyone must make before designing a homeless shelter. Obtaining donations from people or institutions to help homeless who have no intension of "getting back on their feet " is not easy. And if we really want to help this group, what would their shelter and their program look like?

We have discovered over the years that many homeless are reluctant to live around other people. They fully intend to live alone in the wilderness and, "Keep away from those other crazy homeless people!" To those folks I say, "Okay, but we have a warm fire and a big lunch going on tomorrow. Why don't you just drop by and spend a few hours in the day getting to know the others? You can go back to your tent to sleep at night."

This approach has pulled in some, but not all of the chronics. There is no way they can be forced into your shelter. They will come only when they decide that what you have to offer beats living alone in the "jungle". Always remember that if 40% of all homeless need mental help or are substance abusers, maybe 70% of the chronic have the same problem.

None of this answers the question of why would we help the chronic homeless in the first place? Each community must answer that question for itself, but their presence cannot be ignored by denying that chronic homeless exist. Assuming that you want to build a shelter for this group, the question becomes what are their needs and what do they require?

Their needs are simple and straightforward; protection from the elements, warmth, food, transportation to appointments, clothes and friendship, but not too much interaction with others. This pretty much reflects Maslow's Hierarchy of Needs published in 1954 in his book, Motivation and Personality. He defines basic human needs as air, water, food, clothing, shelter and protection from the elements.

Their needs seem to be simple, mostly I think, because they have been denied access to their more advanced needs like self-actualization. Most chronic homeless that I have known are happy to have their basic needs met and not have to do anything in return. It is important to understand this.

Our society typically does not. It is the belief of our culture that we all should strive for more, for the ultimate goal of financial independence, the "American Dream." Anyone who is not interested in achieving this dream is considered by many to be un- American or anticapitalistic, neither of which is acceptable in our community. The question is, how to provide these basic needs while somehow encouraging the typical chronic homeless person to return to self-sufficiency and learn to pull his weight in our culture? The more important question is, why is it necessary that anyone be forced to live our way of life if he doesn't want to? We must develop a plan and build a facility that will take these issues into consideration.

Our experience has been that, while the chronic homeless typically do not want to live in a dormitory setting, they do like having their own small building or private tent. More about this later.

The following data was obtained in a survey conducted from September 2014 through January 2015, made by the Marbut Consulting Company of San Antonio, Texas under contract with Placer County, California. The data applies only to Placer County but since they are the county just north of El Dorado County, I believe that the results and data of the survey maybe applicable to us. I show them here with thanks to Dr. Marbut and the officials of Placer County who have published the survey in the Marbut web site. The comments after each are mine and indicate how the survey results fit with experiences in El Dorado County. The results of the survey are compilations

of responses from interviews with homeless people living on the streets in Placer County.

Triggers of Homelessness

Males

- 50-60% of homeless individuals have major mental health issues. It would be interesting to know how "major mental health issues," are defined and how that number compares with the population as a whole.

- 70-80% of homeless individuals have a substance abuse. As well as the previous comment, it would be interesting to know if homelessness caused the abuse or visa versa.

Over 90% of homeless individuals have at least one or both of these issues. This seems a bit high in our experience.

Job retention.

I assume this mean loss of a job caused homelessness. If so at what percentage?

Females

- Add domestic violence. Again a percentage would be interesting. Add financial hardship caused by divorce/breakup.

- Same as above. **In my opinion, add:**

- Medical or other bankruptcy causing loss of home.

- Unwanted pregnancy.

- Release from jail

- Prior foster care

Placer County at First Glance

The following summaries given in the report based on interviews with homeless people in Placer County that have application to El Dorado County:

- The county lacks connectivity and interaction (no county plan)
  o Same for El Dorado County
- Usable/actionable data in the county is very sparse
  o Same for El Dorado County
- Decisions are based on anecdotes, not strategies.
  o We have no idea on what basis decisions, if any, are made.
- "Policy" is tactical not strategic.
  o Our county has no strategy, tactical or strategic.
- Adult chronic homelessness is a major problem and is getting worse.
  o Same for El Dorado County
- There are major gaps in services for adults.
  o Same for El Dorado County.
- 540 individuals are homeless in the county.
  o A reliable inventory has never been taken in our county but 540 seems to be a bit high.
- Chronically homeless 40% (60% transitional)
- Severely mentally ill 30%
- Chronic substance abuse 32%
- Domestic violence victims 28%
- Veterans 8% (A real tragedy)
- Prior foster care 7%

- Males 61%
- Females 39%
- Single adults 86%
- Children 14%
- Policy decisions should be made on hard facts, not anecdotes
  - o Amen!

Questions asked the Placer County homeless

Where did you go to high school?

- In the county -34%
- Other California counties - 44%
- Other places in the U.S. - 22%

Is your family from the county?

- Yes-50%
- No-50%

Before becoming homeless, did you have a job in the county?

- Yes-55%
- No-45%

How long have you lived in the county?

- More than five years - 67%
- One to five yeas -21%
- Less than one year - 12%

Did you become homeless in the county?

- Yes-83%

- No-17%

How long have you been homeless?

- Five or more years - 26%
- One to five years - 41%
- Less than one year - 34%

2009-2015 Increase in homelessness

- Rate increase - 18.3% per year average. (Over 20% in 2015) compared to 14% increase in population during the same period. The survey reached the following conclusions that are true for El Dorado County as well:
- A homeless shelter should be open 24/7 to keep homeless off the streets during the day.
- A facility should house eighty people and include a complete range of services to aid the homeless.
- Reducing street level homelessness is almost a science.
- Adult chronic homelessness is the elephant in the room.

The following is a summary of an article that appeared in the Sacramento Bee on July 25, 2015. On a single night in late January 2015, the following homeless count was made in Sacramento County.

Homeless found in survey:

- 2659 Total
- 5% increase sine 2013
- 1711 living in shelters
- 948 living on the streets

- More than 1000 suffered from mental illness, chronic substance abuse or both
- 38% of above
- More than 300 were veterans which are 11% of the above

Point in Time homeless counts have been made in El Dorado County in the past also but their accuracy has been put in question. Many homeless don't want to be counted and they retreat into our hills when the counters come around. It is still interesting to compare the numbers in Sacramento County with those in Placer County.

CHAPTER FOURTEEN

Don V.

Don Vanderkar

D on Vanderkar was born on a small dairy farm in Denair, California. He spent most of his childhood in nearby Modesto, with the exception of about two years as a small child when he lived in Alameda where his father worked in the shipyards during World War II. Don graduated from Modesto High School and Modesto Junior College and then attended the University of California, Berkeley where he graduated with a degree in Civil Engineering. While at Berkeley, he met his future wife Peg McClure.

Don and Peg have enjoyed over 50 years of marriage and raised three biological children and one foster daughter who they later adopted. They now have six grandchildren. They also enjoyed hosting four exchange students from Germany and one from Chile. They devote their lives to social service and church activities and love to travel.

Don began his engineering career with the City and County of San Francisco on the Hetch Hetchy Project. The project, situated in the high Sierra Nevada Mountains and partially within the Yosemite National Park, involved the construction of facilities to transport water from Hetch Hetchy Reservoir downstream to the site of a new powerhouse. The powerhouse

connected to pipelines conveying water to the San Francisco Peninsula. Don's many duties included overseeing the drilling the eleven mile Canyon Power Tunnel, construction of connective facilities at the foot of O'Shaughnessy Dam and layout of the Canyon Penstock

After two years of work with the City of San Francisco and Peg's graduation from Berkeley, Don accepted a position with Contra Costa County Water District in Concord, California, where the newly married couple settled.

Don's new job as Associate Engineer involved designing and constructing pipelines, pumping stations and reservoirs. During this time, Don completed requirements for the California Registered Engineer license. He worked 15 years for the Water District and moved through the ranks to become the Chief of the Treated Water Division, a position involving managing the treatment, storage and delivery of potable water to over 40,000 homes. After serving seven years as the Division Chief, Don applied for and was selected in 1979 to be the General Manager of the El Dorado County Irrigation District (EID) in Placerville, California.

EID provides irrigation and potable water to District residents. It also provides wastewater treatment to portions of El Dorado County. At the time Don took this position, EID was being audited by Federal inspectors related to allege miss use of funds and faced multiple cease and desist orders from two departments of the State. Elections to the EID Board of Directors were major local contests. Later, during Don's tenure, residents sought to recall several members of the District's Board of Directors. While in this position, he also served as General Manager of the South Fork American River Hydroelectric (SOFAR) project. This $500M project presented complex funding and permitting concerns and generated significant political issues. Don's more

than two and one-half years of employment at EID were high profile, dynamic, challenging and rewarding.

Upon leaving EID, Don was hired by the then Aerojet General Corporation where he worked for 20 years. The starting position of Manager grew into Director of Environmental Programs. He spent the first ten years working to remediate ground water and soil contamination at the 9,000 acre Aerojet Sacramento facility. The second decade was spent directing investigations and remediation projects at Aerojet facilities in Southern California, including Azusa and Chino Hills. Aerojet faced regulatory actions by State and Federal regulatory agencies as well as numerous lawsuits. Don provided expert testimony in numerous legal cases. Upon retirement from Aerojet, Don worked for four years as a private consultant and served as an expert witness on numerous lawsuits.

Private life after retirement includes enjoying being a grandparent, serving on several non-profit agency boards (including Hangtown Haven), volunteering as a Court Appointed Special Advocate, serving on local and regional church committees, and travel with his wife, Peg.

Don has been working with the homeless for many years. He began volunteering with people without houses about six years ago when he helped with a winter shelter provided by the Seventh Day Adventist Church in Camino. Don spent evenings and nights with homeless people at this facility for portions of two years.

When Hangtown Haven began operation in Placerville in 2012, Don volunteered to work with the residents. His work and responsibilities continued to expand for over one year and until the time the City of Placerville shut down the shelter.

I soon became aware of Don's capabilities and approached him to be a member of the Board of Directors of Hangtown

Haven Inc. He accepted and has been on the Board to the present time serving as Vice Chair and often as acting secretary. His skill and devotion to helping the homeless has been an inspiration to all of us.

Following the closure of Hangtown Haven, members of local churches establish a consortium of churches to operate a Nomadic Shelter program. Five local churches opened their doors and allowed homeless people to sleep on pads in church facilities. Don dove in and volunteered to monitor these operations at three of the churches.

He also became part of the managing group that coordinated the Nomadic Shelter program. This involved establishing procedures, purchasing pads, blankets, etc. and purchasing vehicles to transport people. Hangtown Haven became the fiduciary corporation (501 C 3) to assist the Nomadic Shelter program. Don is now leading the effort to locate a site for a permanent homeless shelter in El Dorado County and is well known in the community for his devotion to helping the less fortunate in our society.

CHAPTER FIFTEEN

The Beginnings of a Shelter

In early 2012 I became involved with the Placerville City Council because I sensed that some key members might be interested in helping the homeless. I met with the then Vice Mayor, Wendy Thomas (her present name) to talk over what could be done. I was encouraged by her comment that asked in effect, "Art, what can we do to help our homeless population?" I was hopeful that finally someone in local government had become interested in helping those who need it most.

Wendy is my neighbor and once raised her two girls in the home my wife and I had purchased in 2003. She and I had talked from time to time and were beginning to find that we had more things in common than I had thought. When she had previously announced to me that she was running for city council she asked me to support her. I agreed and offered to hold coffee klatches on her behalf to introduce her to our friends in the city. Her campaign manager was my old friend and homeless advocate Peter Wolfe.

As a side issue, the county Democratic Party had asked me to run for city council a few days before her announcement, and I was in the process of considering it when we talked about her running. A church acquaintance,, Carl Hagan, had also just announced that he was running for the council. This plus my age made it easy for me to decide not to run.

In the late spring of 2012, Wendy and I sat down on my back deck to discuss what we might do with the city's support to house and help the homeless. She called my attention to the city's Housing Element Report that had recently been completed. On a page near the center of the report it stated that there was a piece of property along Upper Broadway that would be ideal on which to build a homeless shelter. She also

stated that she had been in contact with the property owner, and he had been agreeable to considering the use of part of it for a homeless shelter. She invited the city department heads, me and the property owner Mr. Barry Wilkinson, to a meeting to discuss the possibility of using part of his property on Upper Broadway on which to build a homeless shelter.

It was a very productive meeting and the mayor finally said, "Art, why don't you meet with Mr. Wilkinson next week on his property and see what you can do with it?"

I turned to Barry and asked, "What time tomorrow do you want to meet?"

That brought a chuckle from everyone and illustrated how different it was to work for the city or work for industry. Government employees tend to like to talk a lot "next week." Those of us who have worked in the private sector tend to want to get things done yesterday. Being a Gemini I am probably worse than most in that area.

Barry and I walked his property the next morning as he showed me the area that he was planning to give to us to build a shelter. It was an old fire road running off of Upper Broadway across Hangtown Creek and up the side of a steep mountain. Although the road was not steep itself, the mountain on both sides of it were. We fought our way through the blackberry bushes, poison oak and thick underbrush. It was a mess but had possibilities. I met with Wendy that afternoon.

I reported that, "It is not ideal but I think we can make it work. Let me make a drawing of how a 'tent city' would look on the site and go from there. The one thing that will make it work is a good bulldozer operator, and I know just the man."

Wendy responded, "Okay Art, but remember the city of Placerville does not want to get involved in this project legally or contractually. In other words, you need to form a nonprofit

corporation and be responsible for everything that goes on at the site, including the property lease with Barry and all required insurance. The city will give your corporation a temporary Special Use Permit and you can take it from there." I didn't know what she meant by, "temporary," but I said "Okay, Let's go."

I rounded up two old friends, Jim Ellsworth and Ron Sachs to be my board members and asked Jim to fill out the huge amount of paper work required to form a non-profit corporation. Jim is an absolute expert in the legal and financial aspects of forming and running a nonprofit corporation. He ran the El Dorado County Community Health Center for many years. It took several months, but the IRS finally came back with a letter, "Congratulations. Hangtown Haven, Inc. is now a 501(c) 3 non-profit corporation." It cost us almost $900, but Jim did it on the first try. Russ Reed is an old friend of mine from church who has a wide reputation for being the best 'dozer operator in the county. He walked the site with me in a couple of days, and the more he saw of the property the more excited he became. I laid out my drawing and he scanned it carefully. "I think we can make this work, Art." In a few days, he and his brother Rob showed up on site towing two bulldozers that they had borrowed from a local contractor. They started tearing out the brush, leveling the ground and cutting a drainage ditch along side of the road. They worked for the better part of a week and charged us nothing. They also added a few extra campsites cut out of the side of the toluntain with the skill of surgeons. Before he started carving out these extra sites, I told him that what he was going to do was impossible, and he said, "Watch me!"

HTHI BOARD OF DIRECTORS

**Art Edwards
President, CEO**

Ron Sachs   First V.P.

Jim Ellsworth
Secretary, Treasurer

Don Vanderkar V.P.
HTHI Board Member

Cyndy Salmon
Board Member

Bruce Lacher
Board member

Dan Bitner
Board Member

Don Rake
Board Member

When it was all finished, we had a meeting on site with the county engineer and the fire inspector. That's when the trouble started. The fire inspector said that we had to run the bulldozer for ten feet along each side of the road to clear out the brush for fire protection. This is where the tents would be set up. The city's engineer said, "Wait a minute. If you do that there will be no bushes on the mountainside to prevent mud slides when the rain started." Now we had two important people telling us that we had to do exactly the opposite things before either would approve our use of the land for a homeless shelter. Needless to say, I was very frustrated. We had to find a way out of this dilemma.

Fortunately, Russ Reed was standing close by listening to the conversation. "Wait a minute guys. Before you shoot each other. There maybe a way out." He turned to the two combatants. "What if the hillside is cleared by men and women working with shovels and rakes by hand rather than me doing it with my 'dozer? Clearing the ground by hand will leave a residue of ground cover that will prevent slides but will also cut close enough to the ground to prevent fires. The city engineer and the fire inspector looked at each other. "You know, that might just work." Volunteers went to work and soon had the hillside cleared.

We completed the site by building a wire fence around the property, erecting a wooden fence across the front for privacy, leveling spots for tents, connecting to the water well on the property and connecting to the PG and E service on the power pole also on the property. We set up coverings that are used for housing cars, put a fireplace in the center, set up a donated television for showing movies and bought a small pre- assembled building for our volunteers.

It was a beautiful campsite covered with trees that provided shade that lowered the summer temperature by several degrees.

The fire road was covered with bark and perimeter lights set up with fire extinguishers set along the road. We purchased about forty tents, set out trashcans and told the residents, "Okay, this is your home. You'd better keep it clean." With final approval from the city we opened for business in three weeks.

Remember, the area fire chief is your most important ally. He (she) reports only to the fire district board and does not need any logical reason to shut you down. You must get the fire chief on your side. We were very fortunate to have Bruce Lacher as the fire chief in our area.

Previously when we were considering building a homeless shelter on the other side of town, I met with the local fire chief, not Bruce. His one comment that I remember the most was, "I will never permit a homeless shelter to be built in my community." If we had decided to build there, I guess our only option would have been to initiate a lawsuit against him and his fire department for malicious obstruction or something like that.

The Hangtown Haven campsite was completed and was ready to be occupied by August 1, 2012. It was exciting to see a home grow out of the tangled mess of trees and brush. Here was a place where men and women could live together in warmth, security and in the midst of a loving family. It was a combination of tents, plastic covered common area, fences, portable toilets, a parking lot, garbage collection bin and pre- assembled office building from Home Depot. We started taking in residents, and they immediately elected a ruling council who began work on a set of rules.

It is important to state with all honesty and with much appreciation that Hangtown Haven would not have been possible without the active support of the vice mayor, Wendy Thomas. She was the first city or county official who stepped up

and supported Hangtown Haven in its bid to build a homeless shelter. No other community official was willing to take the responsibility of providing a shelter for our homeless population. I want the record to be clear about how much we owe her for her courageous stand to help the less fortunate in our community. She and I had a few minor differences and my speed in getting things done seemed to have dismayed her at times, but I have told her and will continue to say to whomever will listen that she is the sparkplug that made the Haven a success.

I finally realized what the city meant by "temporary" in the Special Use Permit when she notified me that the Haven would be closed in ninety days. Its closure had nothing to do with its success, because it was soon obvious that it was a roaring success. Was it for political reasons? We will probably never know.

The Reed Brothers clearing the sleeping Area

Clearing the Brush and Poison oak

Vice Mayor Wendy Thomas

CHAPTER SIXTEEN

James A.

James Adkins

James learned as an early teenager that if he wanted things in life he would have to earn them. He began by working as a dishwasher, but he also wanted things like a high school diploma and his own place to live. In short, he wanted to be an adult.

After a few years of working hard at school and his job, he was able to achieve both. Unfortunately, having his own place at such a young age brought a partying lifestyle including lots of drinking and drugs. However, within a few years he became a kitchen manager.

For the next fifteen years he was a very successful functioning addict/alcoholic in some high end and successful restaurants. He eventually burned out working in the food industry although he always worked hard. He learned many different trades and always managed to be able to support himself and his addictions, although he had a few setbacks, which forced him to move back home. At one point he even moved to Catalina and found work thinking that he was in paradise and would never leave. Yet he managed to screw that up too.

His addiction to drugs outweighed his alcoholism and he got caught up selling drugs in order to support a habit that was controlling him. For him there was a definite thrill factor and he was good at it until he got caught. The consequences of that arrest made him rethink his destructive choices.

James finally decided that he needed to stop. One of the options he had available was "Drug Court". It was an eighteen-month outpatient program, which included frequent random testing, case management etc. He also went to everyone he knew and told them that he was in this program and truly wanted to stop using illegal drugs. He told them that if they were really his friends they wouldn't sell, give or share anything with him, no matter what he might say to the contrary. He cleaned up and graduated from the program and has never used an illegal drug since.

Unfortunately, his alcoholism returned replacing his whipped drug addiction, and he started working real jobs again. His family was really worried about him and asked him to move home wital jobs again. His family with his sister and brother-in-law. He worked for room and board for a few years until he finally moved into his own place.

His alcoholism peaked and took over his life. He fully intended to eventually drink himself to death, but it seemed that God had other plans. He was a blackout drunk by this time and became incarcerated for just under three years. During this time he realized that this happened for a reason and that he was meant for something more.

He focused on bettering himself, working on his physical, spiritual and mental well- being. Just before his release James found out that his friend Ken would be going to Placerville, CA, a place where he had never been, and where he knew no one. Someone told him about Hangtown Haven, and he decided that he needed to find a way to live there. One day he walked into Hangtown Haven and asked if he could become a resident. He was accepted, and I soon recognized his abilities after the board asked him to join them. He quickly rose to second in command and has always done extremely well in working with both the homeless and the community.

CHAPTER SEVENTEEN

Organizing a Homeless Shelter

At the beginning, we had to decide how Hangtown Haven would be run. The camp was physically beautiful, but that would mean nothing if the people in it could not govern themselves effectively. Most people, including many in the city government, insisted that homeless people must be tightly controlled, told what to do and kept on a short leash. One experienced member of my board said, "You know this will never work. The homeless residents will fight, argue and not get along with each other. You will have to call the cops every night." None of this made sense to me, so I decided on a different approach.

Now, for the second time in my life I was completely in charge, president and chief executive officer of a corporation. Some tyrant executives I have worked for used to say, "I have waited all my life to be the boss, and I am now that I am in charge, everyone will do exactly what I want." I was encouraged to do just that, but my experience, and my father had told me something different. I remember my father saying, "The person who does the work knows how to do it best." Here was a good opportunity to see if he was right, so I turned the responsibility of the shelter completely over to the homeless residents themselves. When I told the city fathers of my plan, they just threw up their arms and asked, "Are you completely out of your mind?"

I first told the residents to select a governing board and elect one as president. Then I sat back to watch the fur fly. They first elected three men and put a woman in charge. I reminded them that they should make no decisions without getting all of the board to agree. Their hardest decision was always who to discharge from the shelter because of some misbehavior, so first

they had to write up a set of rules which they all would follow. My corporate board and I approved their rules and sent them to the city for their review. They approved them, and we were off and running.

At first, the resident board and its president did not believe that they would actually be allowed to make decisions. So they would come up to me and tell me about a decision they had to make and ask me what they should do. At this point I had to be very careful because there and ask tendency in all of us in charge to make a decision and pass it on as gospel. This has to be avoided at all costs.

So, as much as I was tempted to tell them what to do, I made the same response over and over, "I don't know. You're in charge, so it is your decision to make; just let me know what you decide." The only time I asked to be a part of the process was when the decision involved engineering or political issues. Other than that, they were on their Own.

Initially they didn't believe me. They would bring me a problem to solve and then look shocked when I told them to go figure out the solution themselves. After a few weeks of this, they finally came to the conclusion that they were actually responsible for the shelter in which they lived. When this realization dawned on them, they took their responsibility very seriously. Sometimes they would share a decision they had made with me asking if I had any better suggestions. Once in a while I would say, "That guy you just threw out seemed like a nice person. Why did you get rid of him?"

A typical answer was, "You wouldn't want this guy living in your home and we don't want him living in ours!" One of the good reasons to let the residents make these decisions is that most of the homeless had been through drug or alcohol addiction themselves at some time in their lives. They knew

how to spot it, and I became accustomed to hearing "He's been using meth. Look at his face." I had no idea what they were talking about and just shrugged my shoulders. "Whatever you say. You guys are in charge."

Self-respect is one of the missing ingredients in the lives of many homeless. A typical homeless person has gone through losing his or her job, home, family and finally self-respect. No wonder he or she resorts to some addiction. It is exciting to watch the lost self-respect return to each one. This comes when each is given a chance to regulate his environment and make decisions again for his or her own life.

Many homeless are well educated. Becky, a member of our homeless board, had one year of law school before she lost her mother and home. She learned to make good decisions again after a few weeks of wrestling with deep depression and grief. The board saw the level of her intelligence and asked her to be a part of their governing body. She gratefully accepted and became a star member, leading other residents through their own despair and back into living a responsible life pattern.

This leads my story to a remarkable level of success that none of us predicted. Homeless were not allowed into the Haven if they were active drinkers or drug users. As I had mentioned earlier, our board members could often spot a user just by looking at him or her. I, as also mentioned, didn't have a clue. But some slipped through and s were new to sobriety. It was these folks to whom our board members became attached.

Everyone in the camp pitched in to help the addict during those crucial months when he or she was working through withdrawals. One of our residents who had recently joined us would come out of his tent in the morning and say, "Thirty six days without a drink. Hooray!" Everyone in camp would jump up, run over to him and give him a hug and kiss. He would

beam. "Next you have to get through today," someone would say, and they would all sit around the fire on that chilly morning and tell him how special he was and that he was going to get through it. I can still see him beaming as he sipped his first cup of hot coffee and nodded in agreement.

A member of the county mental health agency came to us on one of her visits and shared an interesting story. She told us that their experience with curing people from addiction did not have a good record. "Oh, it was easy to get them off of drugs or alcohol, but the problem was keeping them off. The rate of return to addiction was something like 80%," as I remember. She was shocked when we told her that none of our residents returned to drugs or alcohol as long as they continued living at the Haven. Their comrades wouldn't let them.

It, of course, was more than not letting them begin again. The pressure of your peer group is enormous, and the community bond that came out of the Haven was stronger than even we realized. No one had to criticize a person for taking up drinking again. It was just the thought that you had let down your friends, a thought that didn't need expressing. It was just there in everyone's eyes. No one dared start drinking again. There would be no more hugs, no more, "Atta boy John. We are here with you." The fight out of addiction is neither easy nor pleasant, but when you have the support of forty other people, most of who had been through it before you arrived, it somehow becomes easier and more certain. "I've got to get through this. I can't let them down!" Our county lady left shaking her head.

Looking Up Tent Row At HTH

CHAPTER EIGHTEEN

Early Mistakes

We made several organizational mistakes at the beginning. The first group leader selected by the residents was a woman who had just returned from Iraq. She was an Army veteran who had been in the military police, so I figured that she knew how to lead a group although I had not selected her. As with every leader, I stood back and watched her direct operations. She pitched in and willingly did her part to make the facility livable. But her management skills were lacking.

She made crucial decisions alone and did not consult with other members of her management team. I think that her mismanagement style helped the others to see how important it was to include everyone in the process. She soon left the Haven for reasons that I can't recall, and another person stepped in to take over leadership.

Larry was an ex-sailor and a veteran of Iraq. When he realized that I had been a naval officer and was a veteran of the Korean War, the two of us hit it off quite well. If the reader has ever been around two ex sailors, you know that they spend most of the time sharing sea stories, some real and some not so real. Often in the retelling events seem to get more dramatic each time they are told. In the repeated story, the seas are higher, the winds stronger, (blowing like stink is a favorite nautical expression) and the enemy more present. There is lore of the sea that landlubbers just don't understand.

He listened carefully to me as I explained how our system worked. He was to share a problem with other members of the board and then, together, make a decision. But if there was a disagreement in the group, he was the final decision maker. It was a new experience for him. He was used to commands being

handed down from the bridge. But he soon got the hang of it and, being a basically smart guy, made some very wise decisions. He was another example of a person who should have had a high paying leadership job in industry, but had been caught up in the tragedy of the country's economic recession.

He wound up with a great job as a truck driver with his own rig living in Texas. He Sent Hangtown Haven a check for $25 from his first paycheck after he left. He has dropped in several times since during some of his cross-country hauls to talk over old times and share with us his lifer after graduating". We heard recently that he was involved in a bad accident while driving his rig and was laid up for some time. He has recovered and is driving again.

When Larry left for his new job in Texas, the board's second in command moved up into the leadership role. Ken had watched how things worked when Larry was in charge, and the transition was smooth. He quickly commanded the respect of the forty or so residents and included everyone on the board in his decisions. We had board meetings once a week, and the police even attended to see how things were going. It was the board's idea to invite the sergeant in charge of the area.

Police Sergeant Carl Bialorucki is an amazing policeman who is very concerned about the plight of the homeless. He dropped by several times a week to sit, have a cup of coffee and just chat with the residents. He knew everyone's name, and they all learned to respect the police by listening and sharing their condition with this amazing policeman. Each time he left, someone would say, "Hey, that cop isn't so bad after all."

Becoming friends with, and including the local police in shelter affairs, is not just a great idea, it's a must. It is the same principle involved in including the local fire chief in your

planning, except that the police should be involved daily and should be asked to talk to the individual residents.

The experiences that most homeless have historically had with police have been bad, and it takes a while to get the chronic homeless even to be around a policeman. However, having the police come by and get to know the residents was a great success and reflected on the competence of the chief, George Nielsen. Many opinions changed after getting to know the local cops one on one. A cup of coffee always helps too.

There is a saying that the attitude of an organization reflects the attitude of the person in charge. We found this to be absolutely true in the police attitude toward our homeless community. The man who was chief when we started, George Nielsen, was an extremely competent leader and was dedicated to aiding us in working with the homeless. He showed up at our meetings and often congratulated the residents on the cleanliness of the shelter.

Initially, the chief told us that he had noticed a significant drop in reported crime in the area of Upper Broadway beginning the day that Hangtown Haven opened. George would sit around and talk with individuals while enjoying a piece of pizza or a cup of coffee. The rest of the force reflected his competence.

Unfortunately, he retired in the fall of 2013 and the city selected his successor. The change we saw was immediate. Fewer policemen dropped by to chat and we never saw the new chief at the camp unless he came to arrest someone. This should have been a warning to us of things to come.

The police chief works for the city council and typically reflects its attitudes and priorities. We were beginning to see that the council's attitude toward having the homeless camp had changed. The council members were pleasant to the homeless residents, and me, but trouble was brewing underneath it all.

This trouble showed up in the attitude of the new police chief and the altered attitude of policemen on the best I don't believe that Sergeant Bialorucki dropped by again after chief Nielsen retired and the new chief took over.

Chief Nielsen Enjoying a Pizza With The Residents

The Vice Mayor, HTH President and Police

CHAPTER NINETEEN

Becky N.

Becky was born to a loving mother and an Air Force father, but her father chose not to be a part of her life. At age two she was diagnosed with extreme hyperactivity and placed on an experimental drug program; one of the drugs she was given was Ritalin. At age four her mother remarried and her parents decided to take her off all the medications at once. Her stepfather started to be physically abusive to her and to her mother.

When she was seven a little brother arrived in the family. When she was twelve her stepfather began sexually abusing her which lead to her cutting classes and generally creating chaos.

Her parents bought a pizza business and her mother, suspecting what was going on, began working long hours so she could avoid being home as much as possible. At age 15 Becky was managing a neighborhood pizza restaurant, and at 16, voluntarily went into foster care. She returned to her mom's home at age 17 where she again worked as a kitchen manager at a local restaurant that her mother managed. During this period she also attended El Dorado High from which she graduated several years later.

She soon met a young man who had a daughter of his own, fell in love and married him the following year. Her only dream was to have a family of her own, a loving marriage and a house with a white picket fence. A year after that she gave birth to another girl.

Two years later they built a house and life went along well for about 6 more years. She was a room mother and a girl-scout leader. She struggled with the issues of her abuse but tried to put on the air of normalcy. Then, after she discovered her husband's

second affair, she found out that a close family friend, who she and her husband tried to help out was sexually abusing her three girls. This was too much for her, and she had a nervous breakdown.

Not too long after she recovered she started hanging out at The Sportsman's Hall. At the time long after she recovered the street. She started drinking, learn the play pool. There she pool hallet dating a man who introduced her to meth. She would realize about tenet and star that she had been an addict since she was two years old; the Ritalin had already made her vulnerable.

She dated that man on and off for the next fourteen years spending a good portion of that time using drugs. In 2003 she separated from him and got clean. In 2004 she moved to Folsom to care for her mother who suffered from COPD. In 2005 she got back together with her husband and they got clean together for about a year. In 2008 she inherited $86,000, and they spent all of it in about a year. They then moved back to Placerville living in several houses, but she was unable to break her addiction.

On Mother's day in 2010 she was arrested on a charge of obstruction of justice while mouthing off to a cop and not doing what she was told. That was the last time she ever got high. Those were the five worst days of her life.

She was still trapped living an addictive lifestyle and In September of 2011 she and her husband moved to a mobile home in Placerville. Her mom was getting sicker almost daily and taking care of her was a full time job.

Then on December 4th everything changed forever. On that morning Becky had planned to go to the Christmas Parade, but it quickly became evident that she would be taking mom back to the hospital. Her mom had taken a serious turn for the worse. The police arrived but officers wouldn't let Becky take her mom

to the hospital. Her mom died on the floor in front of her. Life deteriorated steadily for her after that.

I first met homeless Becky when Ken brought her into the Haven one day and introduced her to me. She was obviously very bright and I encouraged the guys to bring her onto the board. They did, and she did more than her share to help those men and women who needed it most. Everyone fell in love with her as she took naturally to the atmosphere and camaraderie at Hangtown Haven. She is still helping the homeless long after she returns to a productive life and has a job, a home and a new husband.

Becky Nylander Green

CHAPTER TWENTY

Building a Shelter

Now let's talk about the different types of homeless shelters available, their advantages, disadvantages, costs, zoning and the design requirements of each. Before discussing each type, here is a list of what I consider to be the requirements of any homeless shelter. The property must be:

- Within walking distance of a bus line
- Zoned in accordance with SB-2 if it is a building to avoid the need of a
- Special Use Permit
- With a water supply line nearby
- With a sewer line nearby, or
- Able to build a septic tank on the property
- (This can be avoided if you can afford portable toilets)
- Adjacent to an electrical (PG &E) supply
- Relatively level and accessible to wheelchairs
- With shade protection
- Close to potential jobs for the residents
- Accessible by road

Homeless Shelter-Dormitory Style

This is a single large building in which any number of homeless can be housed. The residents typically sleep in bunk beds in an open room like a gym, barracks or large dormitory. Anyone who has been in the Army, Navy, Air Force, Marine Corps or Coast Guard knows what I am referring to here. It can be a new building, designed specifically for use by a large homeless population or it also can be an existing warehouse that

has been converted into a homeless shelter. The main advantages of using a building, new or existing, as a shelter are that they can be built with everything a homeless community and supervising non-profit corporation need to operate. For example, a well-designed shelter building should include:

- A commercial kitchen
- Large food storage lockers and refrigerators
- Large common area for eating and congregating with TV and fireplace
- Separate bathroom and showers
- Clothes washing and drying room
- Library for studying and job search
- Separate sleeping area for patients recently released from hospitals
- Office for the non-profit
- Small meeting rooms for individual or group therapy sessions
- Sleeping room for over night volunteers
- Storage rooms for homeless gear and personal belongings
- Heat and temperature control
- Small medical clinic areas
- Check in and control room for volunteers
- Adjacent patio for barbeques and picnics
- Adequate parking area (building code requirement)

The disadvantage of a single building is that it cannot be easily expanded if more homeless show up than were planned for.

Needless to say, such a building and its property will be expensive and must adhere to local building codes and be designed by licensed architects and engineers. Without going into detail, 1 want to discuss one of the most expensive requirements a building like this would have, and that is the requirements for fire and safety protection.

It is now a state law in California that fire sprinklers are provided in the ceiling that automatically opens up when a fire is detected in the building by its heat sensors. The law requires a certain spacing of these sprinkler heads along the ceiling and a water supply large enough to provide all the heads with sufficient water to be activated together. One can only imagine the size of the water supply lines required for a building that houses one hundred homeless people.

The second fire safety requirement is that a fire hydrant must be located within five hundred feet of the building in which people live. And this is five hundred feet along the road, no of the building in which people lit must also be supplied by a six-inch diameter dedicated water Windiess The old saying goes, now we are talking about real money.

I have heard it said by a reliable source that these fire protection requirements do not apply if it is an existing building that has been modified, but I have not confirmed this.

It is now important to understand Senate Bill 2 (SB-2) and its implications in the building of a homeless shelter. For many years counties and municipalities in our state have used their zoning laws to exclude homeless shelters from being built in their communities. In answer to this ruse, the state passed SB-2 in 2007. The bill is thirty pages long and requires, among other things, that all counties and cities designate one of their zones in which a homeless shelter can be built "by right." Each community is required to accept this bill and establish the

appropriate zone. I believe that each county/city was given a year to accept the bill.

El Dorado County responded quickly and established one of its "commercial" zones in which a shelter can be built. The city of Placerville dragged its feet and didn't accept the law until 2012 and then it designated "highway commercial" as its zone of choice. It just so happens that there are only two streets in town with that zoning which are a total of maybe a half a mile long. SB-2 applies to properties with buildings but not with tents. There will be more on that later.

If your county Board of Supervisors has not yet voted to accept SB-2 they are in violation of the law and, I presume, open to a lawsuit. Don't hesitate to threaten them with a lawsuit if necessary. Remember that SB-2 does not require that a county/city build a homeless shelter, only that they must designate a zone in which one can be built by right like a hardware store or pharmacy. If you attempt to build your shelter in a zone other than the one designated to comply with SB-2, you will need a Special Use Permit, a virtual impossibility in building a homeless shelter.

A Tent City

The term "tent city" has bad connotations in most communities, and the term is pretty much self-explanatory. Each homeless person or couple is given a tent in which to sleep. A common area separate tent or building is then added as well as a volunteer tent or small building. The common area tents are really fabric enclosures either 6"x6", 8'x8' or 8'x12' and arranged around a fireplace so that the residents can gather together without getting wet in the rain. Hangtown Haven was a tent city although we never called it that.

We set the tents (8'x10' by 6' high) on pallets covered with plywood to keep rain and running water out. Each plot was leveled for comfort, and the tents were covered with a waterproof plastic tarp. Tents themselves are not waterproof.

A tent city has the advantage of providing a private storage place for each resident and allows each person to sleep alone, all at relatively low cost. This advantage is important to many chronic homeless people.

A tent city also has some disadvantages, one of which is snow. It snowed on Hangtown Haven once during the winter, and the residents ran up and down the line of tents brushing off the snow before it accumulated enough to collapse the tents. They were not always successful, but repairs were easily made.

The main disadvantage, other than the obvious ones, is that tents are not allowed as permanent housing in any county/city building codes. This means that you will need a Special Use Permit to build a tent city for the homeless in your community. Getting a SUP for anything is next to impossible, and one to build a homeless shelter is almost as impossible as building a concrete airplane. We were successful only because the city was on our side at the beginning. Plus we were able to argue that Placerville was founded in 1849 by 10,000 gold miners living in tents, and they didn't seem to mind. But some of them struck it rich. This brings up the question of building codes versus zoning laws. Which takes precedence? The question probably needs to be resolved legally although I would bet on the building code.

Tents at HTH

Individual Wooden Buildings visualize these buildings as taking the place of tents. We designed one 8'x12" building with two built-in bunk beds and mattresses, desk and closet. We built une for display (much to the chagrin of the city) and showed it off to anyone who was interested. It has the advantage of not being a tent but is still governed by the building codes, so a single fire nozzle will probably still be required to be located in the ceiling. Also, most building codes now require that wall insulation be included to protect the inhabitants from the cold. Our little building was built with a single wall. If insulation were required, an inner wall of wallboard or plywood would have to be added.

In terms of fire sprinklers, fifty of these wooden homes built together would not require a water system large enough to handle all fifty going off at once. Sizing the system for one at a time would seem to be adequate because fire is not likely to start in all of the buildings at the same time. The local fire people would have to agree with This.

The wooden building we built cost about $2500 including bunks, mattresses, desk and linoleum floor. However, a price of $3000 is probably more accurate.

The best combination for a homeless shelter seems to be starting with tents and then building individual small buildings, replacing the tents as funding becomes available. Personally, I like this option the best.

8' X 12' Wooden Shelter Building

Homeless Residents Assembling Their Wooden Building

Building one hundred or so square foot buildings seems to be gathering popularity around the country and for good reason. However, people must be aware of the applicable building codes either in the city or county. Even though it's a small building, if it has people in it, it must be built to the same electrical,

fire, insulation, concrete and other requirements found in the building codes. You need to work with the building department on its requirements here.

Apartments

It is my opinion and experience that putting homeless into individual apartments is the most expensive of all the options and has the least benefit for the homeless residents. We helped some of our residents move into their own apartments and found that the first thing they did was hold a beer party in their new homes. The typical homeless person responds very well to having others like him around as in any of the other options. Allowing him or her to live alone is usually inviting trouble. It might work as a second phase option, but it often does not work for those in their initial phase of recovery. It is just too easy to have a party.

The second problem with individual homes or apartments is that many people don't know how to live alone. Planning, buying and preparing food, for example, has never been a part of their lives. This is particularly true for men whose lives have typically been supported by mothers, wives or girlfriends. Before you give a homeless person an apartment, you must be sure that he or she has licked his or her addiction and can survive on his or her own; in other words, someone who is in phase two of recovery.

Leased Homes

Leasing a home for up to six homeless can be done but it has some of the issues mentioned in the previous paragraph plus one very important issue. Our experience here in El Dorado County has not been good. The one attempt we made to lease a home (see Chapter 29) resulted in several homeowners rejecting our attempt to lease their home when they found out

that we would be housing otherwise homeless people. To avoid the problems listed in the previous chapter, I advise putting a "house manager" in the home with the others.

Rotating Shelter

In some areas including El Dorado County, churches have banded together to open their doors, one of them including El Dorado let the homeless sleep in the sanctuary of other parts of the church. Ce nights a week homeless are bused to a different location each night. This program Geesequently, the the street at night but has several disadvantages:

- A fleet of vans or buses is required to transport the homeless
- A number of qualified drivers are needed
- The homeless are destabilized by moving them to a different location each night. They need stability.
- Buses drop homeless off in town each morning to spend the day roaming around
- Transportation takes four or five hours a day.
- Homeless from out of the area are accepted since hometown verification is impossible.
- It is difficult to separate "chronic homeless men" from mothers with small children in rotating shelters.
- A large number of volunteers are required at the shelter including those that spend the night.

It can be done, but I recommend that a rotating shelter system be the last resort; it's better than sleeping on the street if nothing else is available.

Phases

It makes sense to consider helping homeless people in phases as they work back into society and a home of their own. Phase one has several goals:

- Transition out of any addiction.

- Become acquainted with others in your same predicament

- Dedicate themselves to stop worrying about their own situation and begin helping others

- Learn to survive on their own

- Start searching for a job or go back to school

- Stop blaming others for their situation

- Accept personal responsibility for getting out of homelessness

- Learn to share their feelings

As mentioned earlier, many chronic homeless will not be able to complete all of these goals. This is because some have no interest in doing so while others need professional care that a shelter cannot provide. Any of the first three shelters listed carlier will provide the environment necessary to accomplish phase one. When a resident has demonstrated that he or she has accomplished the eight items listed above, it is time to move onto the second phase.

Phase two is living alone in an apartment or home rented by the non-profit Hopefully learning to survive means learning to plan, purchase and cook food. This seems to be natural enough, but it is amazing how many homeless do not know how to cook or maintain a checking account.

At Hangtown Haven we were able to graduate only a very few residents into a phase two living situation. Consequently we

have no data to illustrate its success rate. The few that we have seen have confirmed how important it is that this phase not be attempted until all of the items listed earlier are successfully completed. It is even wise to stay a little longer in the beginning phase to be sure that the resident is truly ready to move on.

A Happy Camp

CHAPTER TWENTY-ONE

Construction Details

The following:

To make Hangtown Haven on Upper Broadway successful, we provided

Water

The property on which the shelter was built had a well that was drilled down several hundred feet to bring up water that supplied the Wilkinson family homes up on the hill. Mr. Wilkinson graciously allowed us to tap into his supply line and provide water to our homeless residents. My water expert provided a water purification system that would guarantee that the well water was drinkable and connected all of the piping at no charge to us. The testing seemed to be unnecessary since the Wilkinson family had been drinking the well water for twenty or so years, but I thought it wise to test the water. I had the water tested for contaminants and it came out clean. The homeless residents truly enjoyed having an infinite supply of clean water for their personal use.

Electricity

A PG & E service pole stood next to the well, and power had been run down it to a breaker panel that supplied power to the well's water pump. I made an agreement with Mr. Wilkinson that if he would let us tap into the pump's power supply, we would pay his electric bill. Our electrician did the interconnection with several new breakers and built a wooden panel along our wall with six double outlets built into it.

This gave the residents the ability to plug in a TV, coffee maker, microwave oven, and laptop computer and allowed

them to recharge their phones. I think they enjoyed having an unlimited supply of electricity as much as they did having clean water. I have to admit to making a mistake at this point. I forgot to ask the city for Admission to connect the electrical supply, and they were not happy to discover it had already been installed. I had fortunately used a licensed electrician that the city knew well and respected. When he took them on a tour of the installation they immediately signed off and praised his work. That didn't keep the city engineer from grumbling at me. Things were happening so fast at this point that I had just forgotten to keep him in the loop. I advise you not to make this same mistake.

Garbage

The El Dorado Disposal Company was more than generous with us. They installed and serviced a large garbage container strictly for our use at absolutely no charge. The lady in charge of their office was very cooperative with us at all times and provided outstanding and friendly service. I shall always be grateful to her and her boss for their generosity

Portable Toilets

Barry Wilkinson's family owned a portable toilet service in the county and were also very generous with us. We rented four porta-potties from them and they gave them to us. and their servicing to us for half-price. One of the three was a handicapped unit that the resident ladies asked if it could be for their exclusive use. So I put a sign on the door, "Ladies Only."

Portable Toilets

**Water Supply on The Right
Electrical Outlets in The Back**

Fireplace

I purchased a metal fire place that had a long stove pipe extending above the surrounding fabric canopy. The fire inspector came by to be sure that the pipe was secured to its surroundings, so that the wind would not blow it over. Green Valley Community Church kept us provided with firewood and the comfort of the common area kept warm by a roaring fire cannot be over stated.

Even when the evening was not too cold, the residents would gather around the fire and share stories that gave them a feeling of belonging that they had not previously had The importance of this area was immense. We are eternally grateful to GVCC for their continual supply of firewood.

Firewood

Television

Someone dropped off a 52" television one day, and it was immediately put to use. We could not get TV reception in the area, but people donated movies that the residents enjoyed watching every night while sitting by the fire and roasting marshmallows.

Office

There was some debate regarding the importance of having an office building next to the community center. But it was soon obvious how important it was. I bought a pre- manufactured shed from Home Depot, and the volunteers assembled it on site. Our electrician connected plenty of power from the breaker panel, and the small office was filled with warmth and light. The volunteers loved it, and we used it as a small meeting room whenever I came on site.

The Volunteers' Office Ground Cover

The road on which the tents were placed was, of course, dirt. It was dusty in the summer and a mud patch in the winter. I ordered several truckloads of small bark, and the residents hauled it up the road in wheelbarrows and spread it out. It proved to be a lifesaver to keep mud and dirt out of the individual tents. Having the bark to walk on was worth every penny we spent on it.

Ground Cover

Fire Extinguishers

We hung fire extinguishers every hundred feet or so along the fence. This made the fire department very happy.

Barbeques

We bought several barbecues that the residents used periodically. They used them often to cook their own dinners on warm evenings, and we had a few big picnic dinners to celebrate our success as the year wore on. It was fun to invite the mayor and the chief of police and share barbecued tri tip and hot dogs with them.

Refrigerators

Someone donated a refrigerator and freezer that we used to keep food cold. People would often drive by and give the residents frozen or cold food that would have spoiled if we had not received these generous gifts.

Van

The most expensive donation given to HTHI beside the bulldozer work was a seven- passenger van donated by Wells Automotive, a used car dealership on Missouri Flat Road. I had made a comment to one of our volunteers from Green Valley Church that she sure could use a multi-passenger van to transport our residents to doctors appointments. In a few days, the owner of Wells automotive called me to come and get our new (2003) Ford van. We were all ecstatic to have this generous gift and used it daily. I put James Adkins in charge, and he took good care of it.

Donations

Local people would drive by and stop in to donate whatever they had. Toilet paper, warm clothes and women's needs were always gratefully accepted. Many times large gifts of food were brought in and left. I remember one time that so much food was donated in one day that we gave what we couldn't use to the Upper Room for its nightly dinner service. The Upper Room provides dinner for anyone who shows up to eat.

Our New Ford Van With James in Orange Shirt

As mentioned earlier, we received and requested no funds from any government source. Everything we did was financed by donations and gifts from churches, non- profits and individuals. Over the fifteen months we were at upper Broadway we received almost $50,000 in donations. All of us at Hangtown Haven are very proud of the shelter we provided without costing the taxpayer a dime.

There is no question that the property owned by Mr. Wilkerson was ideal on which to establish a homeless shelter. The Placerville Housing Authority plan confirmed this. Few properties will have water and power on site waiting to be connected to a shelter. But it does show what can be done when everyone, city governments, non-profits, concerned individuals and numerous volunteers pitch in with a common goal in mind. In our case, there were some big problems to be worked through before success was realized. Beginning a project like Hangtown Haven before getting everyone in the community on board is risky at best. Also, as we discovered, any of your supporters can turn on you at any time and terminate your best-laid plans.

HANGTOWN HAVEN NEWSLETTER
November 1, 2012

As winter approaches, it is apparent that the operation of the Haven needs additional support from the volunteer community. There are times during the middle of the day when extra help is needed to coordinate and supervise the lives of the homeless people living there. Responsible and experienced homeless residents are often gone during the daytime aiding at CRC, searching for jobs or running errands downtown. As a result, there have been periods when no responsible person is available to coordinate activities.

Consequently, we are putting out a call to all churches, supportive non-profits and other individuals to provide volunteers to help us keep Hangtown Haven running smoothly. A team of two volunteers would work together. These volunteers would do the following:

1. Be on site three hours a day, either from 9:30 AM to 12:30 PM, ot 12:30 PM to 3:30

2. PM.

3. The shifts would be five days a week, and not on the weekends.

4. Hopefully, if we have ten volunteers, it would mean one three-hour shift per week. If we have twenty volunteers, it would mean one three-hour shift every other week.

5. An office and a propane heater will be provided to supplement the fire pit for warmth.

6. Most of the shift would be taken up reading or talking with the homeless on- site.

7. Specific responsibilities of the volunteers while on-site would include the following:

    a. Check in new residents from CRC and help them fill out their transfer slip, liability release and list of rules. They will then ensure that these documents are properly stored in each person's file.

    b. Maintain the site census based on new arrivals and departures.

    c. Maintain the site cellphone to use for emergencies and local communication.

    d. Coordinate with on site council members on general issues on site.

    e. Ensure that the parking lot is clear when toilet cleaning, delivery or refuse removal trucks are due.

    f. Coordinate with law enforcement, mental health or parole officers when they arrive.

    g. Call the police, ambulances or other emergency vehicles when needed.

    h. Contact Hangtown Haven board members when appropriate.

    i. Provide access to the fire hose in case of fire.

Please contact Ron Sachs, Shirley Edwards or Janis Carney if you are interested in helping the homeless at Hangtown Haven. Thank You.

Art Edwards,

President

A Vietnam Army Veteran Lived Here

CHAPTER TWENTY-TWO

Reflections Beside The Campfire

A glimpse into the heart and soul of Hangtown Haven
By
Rebecca Nylander (Now Green)

I sit looking around the campfire that I share with my community who are my family. I am reminded of the many amazing stories of which I have been a part. 1 live in a family of nearly 40 brothers and sisters. Many other members of my family have come, shared moments of life and moved on. Some of us have lived together for most of a year. The warmth of the fire reminds me of the warmth of family members resulting from the struggles we have shared. Our family has experienced triumphs and defeats. But mostly I am reminded of the hope that a simple community can create and the support that is offered and the grace received. Love wells up and endures in a population that many outsiders wish would simply disappear. Let me share a little perspective about myself and some of the stories of my family members.

I came here after the tragic loss of my mother and my home. I was a lost soul deep in grief with nowhere to turn. What I found here at Hangtown Haven was a family, a fuith and a horne. Feeling safe with people who cared about me. I could finally get my feet under me. I developed a passion for what Hangtown Haven does and discovered that by caring for others, I could help heal myself. On top of the safety and security here, there is a purpose and a reward greater than I could imagine. I became a member of the Community Council that leads the Haven.

M is a gentle spirit who is plagued with such severe arthritis some days he can barely move. One Saturday we happened to receive an abundance of donations (an extremely rare occurrence due to two local weddings), which were brought to the cang by people in the community. M pulled me aside and mentioned a family living just up the street with two teenage boys. He said they were having a very hard time financially and had no food. M went to talk with this family and about an hour Later the fishes arrived. We were able to fill his car and trunk with food. The man went away in tears and all he said was: "Imagine this help from a homeless camp. I later found out that M tad used his social security money to pay that family's back rent so they didn't lose their home.

R is a jolly soul who served our country in the Air Force in Viet Nam. He struggles with alcoholism but has done better in controlling his addiction at the Haven than ever was able to do surviving on his own. In the past year he has had two open-heart surgeries. The most recent surgery occurred about three months ago and resulted in a stent being placed in his heart. When the doctors opened his chest, they found that R. led 99% blockage of blood flow. As a family we watched and held our breath waiting for bin to return to us, fortunately he did. R always has a witty comment or a somewhat off color joke to offer. But, when appropriate, he's also the first one to say, "Cut the unnecessary hype you guys and be serious."

C is a young man who came to us fresh out of jail. He had been a frequent guest there and was cocky and full of himself. We worried about him, but after he was with us for a while he started to learn what the Haven was about. Consequently, he began to step outside of himself and to take great pride in having a neat, well-kept living area. During the summer he even signed up for college. He is an amazing example of determination who has also turned out to be quite a gentleman. He always walks

one of the ladies to the store or the bus stop to make sure she gets there safely. He has become more humble and always has a smile for everyone.

E is an older gentleman who has experienced more tragedy in his life than anyone should have to endure. He lost his wife and child to a drunk driver some years ago. This was followed by four other tragic losses.

We often hear G screaming with the night terrors from which he still suffers. Gence Imade a living as a taxi driver, however due to the effects of diabetes he is now unable to drive or see well enough to do his own shopping. He is basically unable to leave camp Without escort.

JW is Bi-polar Schizoid-affective. She requires a constant source of outside stability. She also must be watched constantly as her mood can swing drastically from giddiness to sobbing to aggressive behavior. She has found a great deal of support at the Glown Haven and always finds a person willing to listen to her or just hold her if Abe is upset. There seems to be no shortage of comedians when a silly distraction is pooped. She's our Pilisbury dough baby, as a gentle poke to her belly will result in giggling

T is one of our strongest individuals both physically and mentally. He was released from prison after serving fourteen years for a commercial burglary during the three strikes days there serving fourteen years for and away from that experience as and is the most grateful applied to all crimes. He came away from that experience as one of the most grateful and thankful men i have ever known. He volunteers his time and is always willing to lend a hand. If there is work to be done that is where you will find him. T also reminds me that the fastest way for me to have a good day is to start it by putting a smile on my face. About a month ago T suffered a stroke while working for a man that pays fifty dollars a day for ten hours of hard labor, a bit below minimum wage T will take work when he can find it.

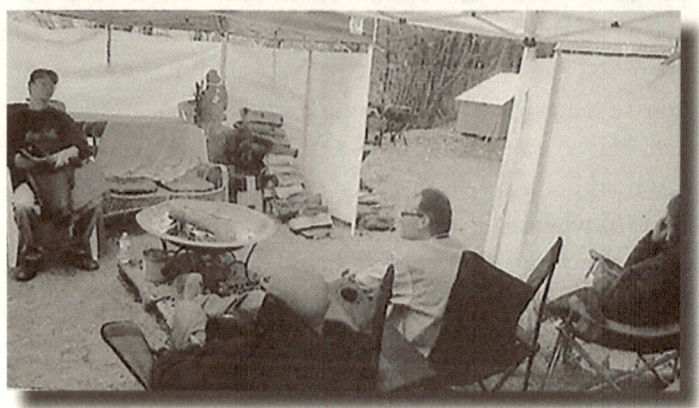

Sharing Stories Around The Campfire

S is a nineteen-year-old woman with a severe learning disability who grew up with a mother who suffered from addiction issues and had a severe learning disability. In spite of this she earned her certificate of completion from El Dorado High School. She has chosen to continue her education by enrolling in adult education classes. Sine loves working with the elderly and has been seeking employment in that field.

JA came to Hangtown Haven after spending three years in prison for an alcohol related offense. If you had asked him four years ago, he would have told you that he planned to die an alcoholic. Now he is a member of the cadership council of HTH. He is deeply involved in service at Green Valley Community Church and has never missed a service. He is a strong advocate for a clean and sober lifestyle and offers compassion when needed and tough love when necessary. He was baptized on August 25th with the other members of the Community Council at Hangtown Haven.

I was a hopeless drunk who suffered from a mental health issue stemming from physical abuse suffered as a child. As I write this, he has now been sober for over 100 days and spends a lot of time helping a friend on his farm. His mental health issues have stabilized and he is now calm and always quick to tease and poke fun, reminding us not to take ourselves too seriously. He is also quick to offer a reminder that this is our home and we must treat it as such.

L. came stumbling into the Haven after being viciously raped and beaten in a nearby illegal camp. She was nearly out of her mind, bewildered, fragile and lost. I will never forget the look on her face when she asked us: "Do you want me?" That is a question no human being should ever have to ask. She is newly, but firmly, committed to her sobriety. In spite of her incredible inhumane experience, she reaches out to every lost soul she can find always with an offering of love and hope. She usually approaches life at top speed and always has a vibrant smile. I cannot go back out into the hills vulnerable and alone. I was baptized on August 25th with others from Hangtown Haven.

K has been and will always be remembered as a part of the heart and soul of IITH. He and his dear friend both came to each other and to the Haven by grace and determination. K who came to Placerville in search of his sister ended up finding

a much larger family. He has offered wisdom, support and leadership to IITH since its inception. K is a staunch protector of our family. He is also the fust to remind us that we have rules and standards and that they must be adhered to. He was baptized on August 25th with the rest of the Community Council for the Hangtown Haven. He is now the leader of our council and loves working with Art.

LR is currently in recovery. He came from a tough background. He has had very little support in his young life and left his family to find his own way. Like many of our residents, he came to us with very little connection to the world around him. He found our family, and became connected to human beings again and to the outside world. He is a gentle giant and I often marvel at the sight of his large framed man embracing a smaller frame of someone in need of comfort and love. He has worked in the field of caregiving and was devastated when a client and good friend passed away.

F possesses a brilliant mind and is a member of the Community Council. He regularly attends Green Valley Church and typically walks out of church every Sunday with a word or phrase of deep meaning for the week. He is the conscience for the Community Council and keeps us focused on our mission and role. He pours his heart and soul into Hangtown Haven and seeks ways to inform the outside world of who we are and what we represent. As our website designer, he asks all interested parties to visit www.hangtownhaven.org.

CD is a young man who suffers from severe learning disabilities and mental health issues. His father committed suicide when he was young and his mother turned to drugs and alcohol. He is another kind soul who, when he came to live with us, illustrated what hopelessness can look like. He is now functioning well in the aura of acceptance he has found at

the Haven. He has even begun to thrive. He is now in school seeking to obtain his GED.

B is an alcoholic who is in recovery. He was recently diagnosed with prostate cancer. When he first arrived, the camp was a bit unsure about this young man. He has turned out to be a great cook, a great friend and great communicator. He relies on our support and friendship to alleviate his fears. He has truly made himself a part of our family. He was baptized on August 25th with others from our camp.

DM is a great kid. Due to an unfortunate accident when he was 17, he has no short- term memory. We often tease him that having him in camp is like the movie 50 First Dates. He is sweet and friendly. If you ask him when he was born, and he remembers that he has an IID he will pull it out and check. He doesn't leave camp without a buddy at his side because he gets lost easily. He is always willing to accompany one of the women on a day of errands so that she isn't alone.

JD is a paranoid schizophrenic who also suffers from severe sciatic pain. There are days that she is totally unable to walk. She relies on us, her family, to check on her and give her food. She also needs to be watched to make sure she doesn't become confused. When she is confused, there must be people around to keep her safe.

DA struggles with depression and addiction. He has found a family who does not judge and has been with him to help stabilize his mental health and aid in keeping him clean and sober. He is helpful around camp and is often quick to offer a grin or a poke in the side.

SR is also Bi-Polar Schizoid-affective. She came to us essentially as a zombie. She had been over-medicated and actually overdosed on esse medication due to an erroneously worded a prescription, we ended up calling an ambulance for

her, and she was hospitalized for two weeks. She is back now and very fearful about her future. She was baptized on August 25th with others from Hangtown Haven.

D is diagnosed as Bi-Polar. She is separated from her family right now while she works on her mental health. She is always quick to play a game of dice with anyone who needs company or a distraction. She has an infectious smile and is always a voice for those who are in need.

CH is a mother struggling to start over. She is clean and sober but has been the victim of domestic violence. She helps prepare meals regularly and does shopping for those who can't go themselves. She has immersed herself in volunteering at Green Valley Church and has participated in several of the Life skills classes offered there.

JC is approaching 180 days clean and sober. If you had asked anyone in Placerville 190 days ago to list the town drunks this gentleman's name would have been high on the list. Now he is a volunteer at the Community Resource Center. He is our camp clown, always laughing and making those around him laugh. He is kind as well as funny.

SM suffers from major depression. She came to us after being in a transition-house for about six months. If you ask her now, however, she will tell you that she is happier than she ever has been. She will also tell you that we live in a place of miracles, a place where there is a home without walls, a family without strife and hope without bounds. She smiles more than she frowns, laughs more than she cries and gives more than she takes.

P was a local business owner for 19 years. She struggles with PTSD and severe allergies that make being inside difficult and uncomfortable. She has a quiet dignity that makes those around want to sit up a little straighter. I look around and I think of those who have come and gone. I think of the miracle that is

Hangtown Haven and the miracles that have occurred here. I pray that miracles can continue to abound in Hangtown Haven, but now we must discuss the reality.

Why have we been told that by November 15 we must shut down the camp and leave this spot we call our Haven? I wonder what the people in power expect to happen. It should be obvious that if our home is taken away, the problem of homelessness will increase, not abated. The decision-makers are taking a solution and turning it back into a problem. The courageous men and women who have fought to come this far deserve better than to be cast aside and forgotten. They have fought incredibly hard and appreciate every ounce of support they have received along the way. We pray that Everyone who has supported us or wants to stand with us will join together and help find an answer. Four weeks is a short time for a miracle to occur that will keep our home alive and our family together.

There is no logical reason that we can identify that would justify closing Hangtown IHaven. Is the reason that we have become so successful, that we have taken derelicts off The street and brought many back from addiction? But that doesn't make sense. If we had failed or made the homeless situation worse, closing our camp could be justified. There is a lot in life that I still don't understand.

A Clean, Well Kept Common Area

CHAPTER TWENTY-THREE

A Fantasy

Hangtown Haven was more than a place. It was an idea, a dream, and a fantasy. It was more than a shelter. Yes, it was a place, but more than that, it was living proof that human beings in the depth of despair and at the bottom rung of their lives can share what they have with others who are in the same phase of life's worst crisis.

In our society, life is mostly a zero sum game. In order for me to win, you must lose. The Haven was just the opposite. Each person's worth depended on the help that person gave to someone else. "No one becomes enlightened until everyone becomes enlightened." Forgive a paraphrase of Buddha's famous quote, but it rings true when the people around you have no other course, when they have no home, no car, no joh, no self respect, no food and no prospects. It rings true when each resident suddenly realizes that there is someone sitting with you beside the fire who needs your help, your love, and your acceptance. Maybe just a hug will do it tonight, but you know that that person has not received many hugs in his life and it will be up to you to give him or her a hug and support every day.

The Haven succeeded because no single person was more prosperous than the others. It is more than just sharing material goods. Residents had their owa tents, their shared common area where they shared meals and life, access to all the water they wanted, all the electricity they needed and all the food they could eat. What more could they want? Imagine a group of people who had worked their way out of addiction and then turned around and helped their neighbors overcome theirs. "No one reaches heaven until everyone reaches heaven."

As mentioned earlier, one day the residents heard of a poor family living down the street that was hungry. They rallied to gather all the food they could find in camp, borrowed a car from one of the volunteers and delivered several days' rations to a family in greater need than they.

When the father came to the door to see who had rung the bell, he was astounded to see several homeless men and women from Hangtown Haven offering him and his family several boxes of funds to feed his family. He was heard to remark as the residents returned to their car, "My God. All this from homeless people who have almost nothing of their own."

At the beginning of the Haven we had a particularly attractive young lady as a resident who had recently become homeless. She told us that her landlord had insisted that she have sex with him or he would throw her out of her apartment. She refused and found herself out on the street. One day she was sitting around the fire getting wan when a stranger walked into camp off of the street. He was immediately attracted to our cute resident and began to make a play for her. He didn't notice that our resident boxer was sitting nearby watching the event. He immediately jumped up, put himself in front of the aggressive newcomer and clenched his fists. He was a short man but extremely muscular. He told the intruder that his life and well-being were in extreme danger if he didn't leave the area immediately. More importantly, if he ever came back his existence would be terminated. He put his nose in the face of the stranger and it was obvious that he meant it. The stranger turned and walked out of camp and was never seen again. Word spread fast that all women were safe in Hangtown Haven.

The residents owned nothing in the camp except the personal gear that they could carry on their backs and stow in their tents. The shelter was there for their use as long as they wanted it, but the community, not the individuals, owned it. Groups like

this were very common in Christ's time and during the Middle Ages. Even today in other parts of the world monks in orange robes go out into the world every morning from their common residence to beg for food to keep them alive, so that they can worship God in whatever way they wish.

The operating system of Hangtown Haven was not established at the beginning. We weren't sure what would happen when forty homeless residents were thrown together to survive on their own. Our first idea was to build a shelter and then worry about how it should be run later. Maybe if we had known more about human nature it would have been obvious. But its imminent success was a big surprise.

One day a young woman stumbled into camp looking disheveled and bruised. She had no belongings or clothing other than what she was wearing. Becky met her at the entrance and took her under her wing. She had been thrown out of her home by her husband and, not having heard of Hangtown Haven, headed for the hills just to find a place to sleep.

Unfortunately, she was discovered by a group of men and was brutally gang raped the previous night. Someone told her about Hangtown Haven and she stumbled into camp, beaten, raped and with all of her meager belongings stolen. Through tears he asked Reeky if she would be welcome at the Haven. Of course she was more than welcome, and everyone in camp pitched in to assure her that she would be safe and could live in a tent of her own with several strong young men standing by all day and night to insure her safety. In a few weeks she had made significant headway and was well on the road to recovery when the city shut the Haven down.

People are smarter than we often give them credit for. Of course there are exceptions, but the community will often take care of these exceptions. Sometimes they are too far into

addiction to be brought back, but the residents tried again and again until they could see no hope. At that point the offender was asked to leave, but they were told that if they wanted to try again, they were welcome to come back. Sometimes it took several tries for the hardcore to make it. And it took time, the one thing, as it turned out, that we didn't have much of.

Looking at the Haven during its heyday was deceiving. It was just a group of tents and a common urea, with people scurrying up and down the pathway. Many were sweeping out their tents, raking the ground cover, picking up trash or talking with someone in need sitting at the fireplace. Nothing unusual you say. True, But the heart of Hangtown Haven was in the otherwise homeless people who lived there. Its magic was in his or her dedication to each other, to the fantasy that someone cured.

"I am not moving on until everyone in this camp makes it," was a fantasy that seemed to define the residents of Hangtown Haven.

CHAPTER TWENTY-FOUR

Ninety Days and Out

When we were negotiating with the city government to build Hangtown: Haven or Upper Broadway in May, 2012, the vice mayor told me on several occasions that it was an experiment that would last only ninety days and then be shut down. I completely misunderstood her and thought she meant that if it were a failure, as most people believed, it would be shut down after ninety days. I naturally assumed the opposite would be true also, that if it was a success it would be allowed to continue beyond ninety days. I want to be honest about the vice mayor. She never actually said that, just assumed that it is what she meant.

On my behalf I have to say that I couldn't imagine that the city would allow us to stay on Upper Broadway for only ninety days if we could prove that our shelter motel would work. We poured more than $13,000 in donations plus the week's work from the Reed brothers just to get the site operational. If I had actually understood what she meant, I would never have spent that kind of money on the property for such a short stay. But she meant what she said and November 15th was rapidly approaching.

When we were getting organized to build Hangtown Haven, I enlisted the help of an old friend of mine, Jim Ellsworth, for advice and support. Jim had been the leader of the El Dorado County Community Health Center and had a great deal of experience in dealing with the political power in the county. When I told Jim that the vice mayor and initially approved of our plan to build a homeless shelter on Broadway, he looked at me for a few seconds and then replied, "Art, you know that somebody has made a terrible mistake and you are going to pay

for it." At first I didn't understand what he was saying, but it didn't take long to figure it out.

The obvious people in charge, the mayor and city council, apparently do not run our community. I can only assume that this is probably true in other counties around the state. There appears to be a group of influential people in the community that pull the strings and determine who gets elected and who does not. Jim was apparently telling me that the group that was really in charge of our city does not approve of a homeless shelter and would eventually squash it through our elected officials. I would soon learn that my old friend Jim was absolutely correct.

The ninety-day period was due to expire on November 15, 2012. As the date approached, I began to realize that the city leaders fully intended to close us down and return the residents to living on the street in the middle of the winter. Nothing I said seemed to have any effect. So, with only a couple of weeks to go. I asked the vice mayor to have a meeting with us in one last attempt to change their minds. She graciously agreed.

The meeting was held on the fourth floor of the city offices and all the city's leaders were there including the vice mayor. I admit pulling out all the stops and bringing along four homeless residents of the Haven to speak at the meeting. I opened things up by introducing the four and then I shut up and let them do the talking, explaining why it was necessary to let the Haven stay open.

Larry Allum, the Haven's elected leader, summarized at the end and made an impassioned plea with tears in his eyes. When he finished, there was silence in the room as all the city employees in attendance looked at each other. Finally, obviously impressed, the vice mayor said in effect, "Okay. We'll let you stay one year and then close it down." I cheered.

There are those who might say that I played dirty pool by bringing in three men and a woman who had no place to go if we had to close down in the middle of the winter.

But what they said was real, and the city had to face up to the consequences of their action. They were tired of listening to me plead with them, and I'm sure they were not expecting four articulate and intelligent homeless people to present their case so competently. The vicemayor reluctantly agreed, so we walked out with smiles on our faces and returned to tell the other forty residents that they could stay for another twelve months. We all celebrated that night.

The most important result of our first ninety days was that the operation of the shelter was so unexpectedly successful. All of the city employees and administrators admitted that we had the correct formula for running a homeless shelter. The vice mayor had told me from the beginning that the Haven was to be an experiment only. "An experiment in what," I asked? No one had an answer. My experience in experimenting is that if it is a success, you keep it going or expand it. I was never trained in city polities and could not bring myself to believe that being a roaring success meant that we would be closed down. Little did I know.

Getting Camp Organized

CHAPTER TWENTY-FIVE

Rules and Regulations

A ll Hangtown Haven residents were required to agree to the following rules:

Hangtown Haven, Inc.

To ensure a safe and equitable place to live while I experience my transition to a better, I agree to abide by the following:

- No open containers of alcohol or drugs or outdoor/ public intoxication while at Hangtown Haven. If you are found to be under the influence of drugs? alcohol, you must leave the camp.

- ZERO TOLERANCE FOR STEALING. If caught, you must immediately leave the camp.

- No fighting that causes injury to yourself or others.

- Cooking fires and smoking are allowed only in designated areas.

- Everyone is responsible for trash pick-up and keeping the area clean. If your chore is reassigned due to your failure to complete it, you will be "written up'. If you receive a second 'write up' you will be asked to leave for 24 hours. A third write up' will result in re-evaluation of your eligibility to stay at the camp. Failure to sign a 'write up' results in a 24-hour notice to vacate the premises. Quiet time starts at sundown and ends at 8:00am. If excessive noise occurs after quiet time, those involved will be written up.

- No overnight parking. No loitering in cars in the driveway.

- No personal property is to be let in the common arca. Property left in this arca after bedtime will be discarded. No rolling cigarettes on the picnic table.

- No children are permitted at Langtown Haven. Registered 290's are not allowed in the camp. Overnight guests are allowed twice a week, but not on consecutive days.

- No pets are permitted at Hangtown Haven belonging to guests and visitors.

- Residents are permitted to have service dogs.

- All tents and sleeping bags at the camp are the property of Hangtown Haven. Inc.

- If guests have gone more than 3 days without notifying the Hangtown Haven Community Council, a vacate notice will be posted.

- If law enforcement is at Hangtown Haven due to a behavioral disturbance or arrest warrant of your doing, you will be permanently removed from the camp.

- The Hangtown Haven Community Council reserves the right to permanently remove a guest from the property at any time for any reason.

I understand that I am a guest of Hangtown Haven and that any violation of the above rules could lead to immediate eviction per Civil Code Section 799.22.

Name: _____   Date: _____

All of our visitors remarked that the campsite was spotlessly clean. How could we keep it like that? However, as we moved into the new year, the city asked that we assign a volunteer to be on duty at all times during the day. We agreed and made an

effort to round up as many volunteers as possible and put Don Rake in charge as volunteer coordinator. He scheduled their times on site and instructed them in their duties.

One of the volunteers, Janis, came to the shelter one day and looked at the tent I had set up for their use. She glanced over at me and remarked, "Art, you're not going to make us stay in this tent all day are you?"

"No, of course not," I answered as I jumped in my car and drove off to Home Depot where I bought a metal building about ten by ten and brought it back to the site. "Okay guys. Here is your new office building. Let me know when it is assembled and I'll get you a couple of desks, chairs and a heater." When it was assembled I asked our electrical volunteer to connect it to the power supply so that it was fully functional. initially provided power through an extension cord, but I knew I wasn't going to get away with that. At the fire inspector's request, we wired it in accordance with the code. Now we had a warm, comfortable place for our volunteers to congregate each day.

Raising The Flags Every Morning

CHAPTER TWENTY-SIX

Reality

Becky's Reflections in Chapter Twenty-one just about say it all. Working together, the homeless residents and volunteers had only one goal in mind. It was to create and operate a successful homeless shelter in which they could live in peace and security. I suppose that we were partially motivated by the negative comments we heard from everyone around us, especially from the city government. "Your model can't possibly work. Homeless people will not live together peacefully to create a successful operational model."

It wasn't a slam-dunk. We could just as easily have been wrong. It was a tremendous gamble and if we had lost, the city and the county would probably have said, "There, see I told you so. We can never build a homeless shelter because the residents can't even get along with each other."

I am convinced (my opinion only) that this is the reason that the city council under the direction of the vice-mayor (later mayor) authorized Hangtown Haven to be built. "It was an experiment," she said. It was an experiment that I believe most people in our community had bet would fail causing us to go away and not bother them again. They gambled on failure and were faced with success. Now they were confronted with a crisis,

Reasons Hangtown Haven Must Be Closed Given To Us By The City

1)   If you stay longer you will have to fill out a CEQA application and have it approved by the city. You will never be able to pass CBQA.

People who don't want you around often throw at you the threat of CEQA, the California Environmental Quality Act, a state law that mandates that you not foul the environment. I heard that threat many times during our stay on Upper Broadway and finally confronted the mayor with it. She offered nothing specific but suggested that I talk with the city's new Community Development Director, Pierre Rivas. She said that he is an expert in CEQA and could answer all of my questions, so I called him and went in to have a talk. He and I had been friends and knew each other from his days working with the county. The following is the essence of his response to the threat of the Haven having to "do" a CEQA as I recall it.

Pierre had spent some time on the Hangtown Haven property and was very Familiar with it. Ile said that we would have no trouble getting CEQA approval since we were actually reducing threats to the environment by bringing homeless people off the hillside and together in one shelter. He laughed and said that he would, in fact, be willing to write the CEQA report for us himself and then approve it on behalf of the city. He said that it was a "non issue".

So much for a CEQA treat. I have always enjoyed working with Pierre. He is extremely competent, always brutally honest and doesn't play politics. I have often wondered how he gets along in a government job.

2) The existence of Hangtown Haven was drawing homeless from surrounding counties into Placerville.

We specifically told all our interviewers, the radio stations and newspapers that CRC, our coordinating agency, would accept only homeless people who could prove that they were residents of Placerville when they became homeless. Yes, probably some from out of country probably thought that they could weasel their way into the camp, but I line of only a few that did. Those who were non-residents turned around and went back to Sacramento or Auburn or wherever they came from when they found out that they did not have a home in Placerville.

This issue was blown out of proportion when the new police chief began telling the council that the incidents of homeless encounters increased because of these out-of- towner homeless. I think this was a case of telling the city fathers what they wanted to hear. Chiefs get to keep their jobs longer that way.

Of particular interest here is the church sponsored Rotating Shelter. The city council touted the Rotating Shelter as the alternate to Hangtown Haven as a place for the homeless to spend the night at different churches, I have the highest regard fitr the Rotating Shelter but they do not check the hometown of each of the homeless. Consequently our homeless people tell us that at least ninety percent of the homeless who use the Rotating Shelter actually come from Sacramento. I can't confirm their numbers, but many Sacramento homeless rush up to El Dorado County by the first of November each year to sleep in the various churches in the Rotating Shelter system. The city doesn't seem to care that more out of town homeless are here than were ever here when the Ilaven was open. The city has made up its mind, and that is that.

3) The sidewalk between HTHI and the Upper Room is dangerously deteriorating, is narrow and is not safe for homeless people to walk on and would be very expensive to repair. The location of Hangtown Haven is not appropriate for a homeless shelter.

During the council meeting that shut down Hangtown Haven, a person living in the city rose and spoke to the members. He said that he had lived in Placerville his entire life, walked to elementary school on that walkway, and it was as dangerous fifty years ago as it is today, "Why hasn't it been fixed in fifty years'?" No one on the council answered his question.

Yes, the walkway along Upper Broadway is dangerous and has been for over fifty years. Its danger has nothing to do with having a homeless shelter nearby. Of course the city is afraid of being sued if someone is hit while walking on the pathway. That's understandable.

There are people walking along the path today, and if a car hits anyone the city will be sued. If I were a lawyer I would happily be the plaintiff's attorney. The city is open to big awards now, and there are still homeless people walking from their campsite in the woods up to the Upper Rocra. Blaming the danger of that walkway on Hangtown Haven was a bogus argument.

As for the location, let me quote pages P-32 and P-33 of the Placerville Housing Element prepared by the Planning Commission and approved by the City Council:

Recently-enacted Senate Bill 2 (Chapter 63, 2007 Statutes) amended housing element law to ensure that local zoning regulations facilitate emergency shelters and Jimits the denial of emergency shelters and transitional housing under the Housing Accountability Act. Generally SB2 housing element law regarding land use/zoning approvals as follows:

- At least one zone shall be identified to permit emergency shelters without a conditional use permit or other discretionary action.

Placerville's HWC (Highway Commercial) Zone code section will be amended to include emergency shelters as a permitted use subject to appropriate development standards as permitted under SB 2. The HWC Zone was identified as the appropriate zone to allow for emergency shelters because of proximity to services and a sufficient amount of vacant land within the zone. Placerville's HWC Zone encompasses approximately 290 acres, of which 90 acres are vacant, and provides the capacity to meet the emergency shelter needs of 15 persons. Parcel sizes range from 1 acre to more than ten acres. Most notably, a site located at 1700 Broadway (Assessor's Parcel Number 049:170:031), west of Airport Road, is in a Highway (Commercial (HWC) Zone, uniquely suitable for emergency shelters due to proximity of related services, in approximately 6 acres in area and contains minimal physical or environmental constraints. HWC-zoned sites are generally located along transportation routes, near commercial services. The IIWC Zone allows a wide variety of uses compatible with emergency shelters, including retail uses, and highway-oriented uses such as hotels, restaurants and a variety of governmental support uses. In addition, there are known environmental constraints or other conditions within the IHWC Zone that could render it unsuitable for emergency shelter uses.

Please note the comment that, "A site located at 1700 Broadway is uniquely suitable for emergency (homeless) shelters. This is the exact site that the vice-mayor suggested and the City Council approved for the location of Hangtown Haven. The location was not my idea as I had nox read the city's Housing Elernere and was completely unaware of the property. In summary, after suggesting the site for a homeless shelter as it

appeared in the city's ow, document, the council reversed itself and said that it was an inappropriate location. One wonders who got to them.

4) The temporary special use permit must be re-approved before Hangtown Haven can continue.

A local resident stood up in front of the council and said that his property had a temporary Special Use Permit along Broadway and every year the council automatically renewed it. The same could be done for ours if the council so desired. The city's attorney testified that there was no particular requirement to end the SUP and that the council could do whatever it wanted. No one on the council followed up on that.

During the meeting at which the council shut down Hangtown Haven, two things happened that were particularly reprehensible. The first was that the mayor, my earlier supporter, shut me off during my presentation and told me to sit down because they didn't want to hear me any more. The evening did not include free speech except for those who wanted to shut down the most successful homeless shelter in the state.

The second event occurred when a citizen stood up and said that he knew that the Council had already made up its mind, and there was no use in continuing to present arguments. The vice mayor took the floor, and with great indignation said that he was insulted by the implications of the man's argument. He said that the council members would listen to everyone's argument and then make up their minds.

After everyone's arguments for and against were completed, the council members each presented their own opinions and then they unanimously voted to shut us down.. Everyone noticed that all of the council members, including the vice-mayor, read their summary opinions from pre-written, typed pieces of paper. So much for listening to arguments. Their

minds had been made up when they walked into the room that evening.

The Common Area

CHAPTER TWENTY-SEVEN

Closedown in November

W hy did the city of Placerville close down the most successful homeless shelter in California? The answer to that question is not obvious to the author, and may only be known by the city's elite. The shutdown certainly was not for the reasons given by the okey and outlined in the previous chapter. Each one can be easily rebutted. Only those who actually run the city know the real reason. The council members deny it, but I think that Jim Ellsworth was right. There is an invisible power in our community that controls everything that happens there.

Housing and protecting the forty or so homeless residents cost the taxpayers nothing. No lux money was ever given to us to provide this home. The shelter saved money in police and sheriff's time, probation and mental health and especially at Marshall Hospital where we were able to cut down the use of their emergency room significantly. But our existence must have wrangled or financially threatened someone in power

The reason I feel this way is confirmed by the section of the City Council led by the mayor. They agreed to build Hangtown Haven and then soon turned around and led the effort to close it down and force the huskies to live back on the streets. But what reason could there be for this turn of events? It could have had its source in the bottom line here that seems to exist in almost all business people. There are rumors floating around our community that some influential people have big plans for developing the Upper Broadway area with motels, shops and restaurants. This means that these city power brokers have unlimited control over the members of the council, and the council members are unwilling to admit the truth. I don't know

how power brokers operate, "Shut down this homeless shelter or I will not fund your re-election campaign!" I can only guess

We read every day now that an adjoining county is building or operating a homeless shelter based on our experience. Once El Dorado County was in the lead in provide shelter for the homeless community. Now we›re not even in the running.

The vote to close down Hangtown I Haven was unanimous among all five city council members.

Wendy Thomas	Mayor
Carl Hagen	Vice Mayor
Patti Borelli	Council Member
Carol Patton	Council Member
Trisha Wilkins	Council Member

HOMELESSNESS IN EL DORADO COUNTY

The Benefits of Hangtown Haven.

By: Art Edwards

Who has benefitted by closing Hangtown I Haven?

When The Haven Was Open

1. The forty or so homeless lived in a community all of whom supported each other through alcohol and drug addictions. Approximately 40% of homeless are addicted to something. Everyone was encouraged to get clean.

2. The residents flew the camp flag every day demonstrating pride in community nd country. The

camp provided a safe place to store their clothes and other belongings.

3. It was a safe, clean, dry living environment with toilets, electricity and access to showers.

4. CRC did not permit out of town residents to live there.

5. It was a location that was easily accessible to parole officers, police and welfare department personnel.

6. The location was relatively warm and dry in the winter and cool in the summer.

7. It was easy to take people to doctors' appointments.

8. It was located on a county bus route, close to CRC and the Upper Room.

9. No resident was allowed to panhandle or beg.

10. The residents developed excellent relations with the police, many came to meetings, sat with the residents and visited.

11. It reduced costs of Marshall Hospital emergency care because HTHI worked residents to primary doctors.

12. Regular meetings with AA, drug addiction, medical issues and county mental were held on site.

13. The residents felt responsible for each other's behavior.

14. Women were safe living at the shelter.

15. 11 greatly reduced forest fire risks.

16. No resident used private property as a toilet because they had their own Portable toilets

17. Placerville was famous throughout the U.S. for its homeless shelter, and articles about 1HI1fl were

written in the Los Angeles Times, Mountain Democrat Sacramento Bee.

18. It provided a place for the homeless to be in the daytime without wandering the streets of   Placerville.

19. Local businesses benefited from purchases by residents. The residents spent money locally.

20. They had fresh, filtered well water every day,

21. It was a single location where volunteers could bring lunch and clothes.

22. It got homeless veterans off the street.

23. The residents did not allow Megan's Law offenders to stay.

24. The police chief told us that their arrest record dropped as soon as Haven was opened.
Hangtowa

25. Drug use and distribution was not permitted and was cause for expulsion. 27. The Haven cost the taxpayer nothing. It was funded entirely by private Donations.

Since Hangtown Haven Was Closed

1. The Rotating Shelter takes in most of the IITIH residents between November and April, but   many sleep in the woods or on personal property.

2. The Rotating Shelter has difficulty in providing seven nights a week shelter.

3. Grants and gifts are needed to finance transportation.

4. There is no daytime hangout so the homeless are wandering the streets and searching for places to get out of the rain, mainly because the city has restricted

the use of any building within its boundaries as a daytime hangout for the homeless.

5. Most of the HTH residents who were on their way to recovering from addiction have reverted back to their previous drug and alcohol use since HTH closed.

6. It has been reported that the incidents of emergency room use at Marshall Hospitals have skyrocketed since HTII was closed. This costs the hospital and the public hundreds of thousands of dollars.

7. The threat of forest fires from individual homeless camps has increased dramatically,

8. The police force spends a significant amount of its time rousting homeless from their camps in the woods destroying what had been a great relationship with the

9. homeless. The homeless typically return within a few days. Panhandling and begging has become a problem in El Dorado County,

10. There is no legal place in the community for the homeless to sleep during the

11. Over 90% of Rotating Shelter residents are from Sacramento. summer.

Who has benefitted from the closing of Hangtown Haven?

NOBODY!
Hangtown Haven Residents
Summary July 2012 To Nov. 2013

Total Number of residents	62
Left to:	
Get a job	5
Get housing	20
Enter rehab.	3
Told to leave	22
Other	12
Maximum daily	Approx. 40

**Hangtown Haven's Battle Flag Flew
Every Day At Camp Entrance**

CHAPTER TWENTY-EIGHT

Letter From Chris

I am doing pretty well thank you. It has not been easy since Langtowa Ilaven closed last November. I am now warm, sheltered and get three meals a day although they are small portions, but I am not starving as I once was. I have a nice new pair of boots from CRC and I get to shower every other day. They gave me a Bible, so life and God are good to me now.

I do remember when I first met you all at Hangtown Havea when I was just released from prison wearing my shorts and sandals and walking in the snow. You guys saved my life and are my guardian angels.

I miss our camp at Hangtown Haven very much. Even though I was living in a tent it was like living in a loving family. It was our community. I remember waking up) shaving then running down to the bus stop to catch the next bus to the college.

I was doing pretty well until the camp closed down in November, and we were all evicted by the police. When I tried to live alone in the woods my drug addiction returned, but there was no one around to help me stay clean. I stole some items from a store and was caught in the domino effect of drug usage. At the camp we would try our best to stay away from drugs, although it wasn't easy. When the Haven closed down, we had to pitch our tents alone somewhere in the woods. It was not easy living on the streets again. Some homeless had crystal meth, some were using strictly alcohol, somewhere only on marijuana, but everyone became a victim again when he or she returned to being homeless. In other words, everyone had to pick a substance, and when you are homeless with no electricity and no heat, a shot of alcohol will let you have a nice warmth sleep,

I do miss you guys at Hangtown Haven. I was 20 close to making it this time and hope I will make it next time, if there is a next time. School meant so much to me because I found out that I am much greater than I thought I was. I was leering and it was rather easy. I used to snake a lot of marijuane when I graduated from high school in Novato in 1996. I was the star basketball player too, did homework only once a week and smoked weed every day and finally graduated with a 2.5 grade average. I found out Hangtown Haven that college is fun and learning is fun ton, especially when you quit smoking Happy Thanksgiving everyone!

Chris' letter and Becky's reflections emphasize the most important aspect of the Haven. Everyone supported each other! Any successful homeless shelter must have that component, the encouragement that can come only from residents in need who support each other. Individual homes with six people in them don't have it, rotating shelters don't have it and individual homeless people sleeping on the sidewalk don't have it. Only groups living together under the same roof or in adjacent tents or small cottages with a nearby common area provide the interaction that gives the residents the support they need to succeed, especially through overcoming addiction. This is the critical lesson we learned.

It has been almost three years now since Hungtown Haven was closed down by the city and some of the scattered residents still correspond with us and keep in touch with each other. Some are now living in homes, have jobs and drive cars. They have expressed to me how much they miss Hangtown Haven, and the friendship and fellowship that had developed there. Even the successful ones tell me that they miss their "family".

The Volunteer A Poem

By *Larry Allum*

Hangtown Haven, Resident/volunteer. President of The Council

We do not for fame or fortune,

The exhilarating feeling of success that the accomplishment felt within.

No one knows the feeling, how can you begin to explain?

The roads not paved, the jungle uncharted.

We welcome the challenge open hearted.

The worries, the stress, even the second guess,

Sometimes, even the bite in the ass!

We do because we care.

The hours go by, time does pass

But we will not stop just because they are "bottom class"

We will argue, we will fight, all for what's right.

To help those so they will not sleep on the street tonight

The hours are long, the people are rough,

But we will never say, "that's enough"

For those we help are grateful, the others are just hateful

Maybe one day soon they will change their tune

For those who hate it is never too late

Walk through the door as if an open gate

You will never be told you must wait

There may be a lot on your plate, but it's never too late.

We just need you to walk through that GATE.

Larry Allum, Council President and Ex Sailor

CHAPTER TWENTY-NINE

Back To The County

During the summer of 2013, Wendy Thomas, Cari Hagen and I put together a presentation to the El Dorado County Board of Supervisors in which Hangtown Haven, lac. offered to build and operate a homeless shelter on a county owned lot. The new shelter would cost the county and the taxpayer nothing, as it would all be funded by donations, as was Hangtown Haven on Upper Broadway. The property in question was located on Perks Court just off of Missouri Flat Road. The property was located in the county and not in city limits. The mayor and vice-mayor knew that the shredder on Broadway would be closing in November and were hoping that the county would allow a new shelter to be built in the county and would no longer be up to the city.

I composed a letter to the Board of Supervisors that is enclosed below. My letter was discussed at the next board meeting, but no answer was given to me then and my letter has not been answered since.

El Dorado County Board of Supervisors
August 17, 2013
Placerville, CA 95667

Members of the El Dorado County
Board of Supervisors

As you probably know, Hangtowa Haven Inc. is a local non-profit corporation that built and is operating a shelies on Upper Broadway for the homeless men and women of Placerville. The shelter has proven to be a successful, clean, peaceful and

well- organized encampment for those who would otherwise be camping illegally in the forests, canopy buildings and businesses around town. Unfortunately THIs temporary Special Use Permit expires in November of this year, so we must find another location on which the homeless can live legally.

Board members of HTHI have been searching throughout the city and county for a new location on which to establish a shelter and have found an excellent unused lot This lot is owned by the county and is located on Perks Court adjacent to, and just west of, the county property that is now being leased to United Outreach. The lot number is 32713019, is commercially zoned and is adjacent to the freeway.

Hangtown Haven Inc. respectfully requests that the Board of Supervisors lease the property to it for a five year period at a cost of a dollar a year, so that we can build and operate a homeless shelter as we have done in Placerville for over a year. We have been successful in raising funds and will finance all of the construction work and operational expenses with donations and grants from private individuals, religious and other non-profit organizations. The county will not be asked for any funding, only for the use of this property as a homeless shelter. The following are our plans for the property:

1. An attractive six-foot wooden fence will be built, and tall fast growing trees will be planted along the north side of the property to isolate it visually from travelers on the freeway, the freeway on-camp and the buildings in the shopping center across the freeway. A fence presently exists along the southwest property line, and a ditch and steep embankment separate the property from United Outreach along the east side. The proposed new fence will isolate the shelter from people walking by and will give the residents a sense of security and privacy. In addition, a steel fence will

be built between the United Outreach property and our property.

2. The homeless will initially sleep in tents as they do now, but the tents wäl eventually be replaced with "mini-buildings" in which one or two people can live comfortably. These 8" x 12 buildings will replace the tents as funds become available. These "minibuildings" will have no water or electricity and will be designed and constructed by a local builder. Marc Murray has had twenty-those years of construction experience building quality structures in El Dorado County. The mini-buildings will be sitting on concrete blocks, are portable and can be moved at any time.

3. Occupancy of these mini-buildings will be given to only those homeless who have a job, half time or greater, or to guests who are enrolled full time in college. If a guest has a job, and is living in a mini-building, he/she will be asked to pay rent up to $300 a month. When enough of these mini-buildings are occupied, Hangtown Haven West will be financially self-supporting

4. Water will be provided to the common area from a supply line and a meter box existing on the property.

5. Electrical power will be taken from an existing PG&E transformer,

6. A 20 Feet by 32 feet structure will be built over an existing 20 feet by 30 feet concrete slab to provide a common area where the homeless can mingle for warmth and protection from the elements. It will be heated, lighted, will have TV access, desks and computers for job searching.

7. A 32 feet by 12 feet open shed will be built next to the common building to allow the homeless to gather outside if they prefer.

8. Minor leveling will be done on the property and it will be cleared of underbrush and poison oak. No trees larger than four inches in diameter will be removed.

9. Motion activated flood lights will provide nighttime visibility. They will be directed away from the freeway and on-ramp, so the light will not impact cars.

10. Portable toilets and a dumpster will be provided. One of the toilets will be handicapped accessible making the entire facility handicapped accessible.

11. All power except flood lighting and selected electrical outlets will automatically be turned off at 10:00 PM, and quiet time will be enforced.

The camp will be kept clean and organized, and the boneless guests will maintain order and discipline supervised by their own council and monitored by ITHI volunteers as has been done successfully on the Placerville site. Drunkenness and drug usage will not be tolerated, and residents will be reviewed for residency every six months if they have not found a job or enrolled in college level classes. Only homeless who can prove that they have lived in El Dorado County will be permitted to stay in the camp.

Perks Court is a perfect location for a homeless shelter for the following reasons. It is:

1. A hundred yards from the office of the homeless medical coordinator, Sata Mundy.

2. Walking distance from the El Dorado County Community Health Center and preventative dental care.

3. A few feet from the county bus line that gives residents access to jobs around the county.

4. Walking distance from several restaurants, grocery stores, drug stores. Safeway and Wal-Mart.

5. Close to five churches and within walking distance to Green Valley Church

6. Used and presently serves a purpose for the citizens of El Dorado County.

7. Walking distance to many potential job opportunities.

8. Zoned "Commercial" which is appropriate for homeless use.

9. Separated from nearby residences and schools by open lots

10. A location that minimizes public exposure and encounters.

11. Next to the biking trail providing easy and safe access to Missouri Flat Read and Placerville Drive.

12. Partially shaded.

13. Mostly level.

14. Accessible to emergency vehicles,

15. Unseen from neighbors and the freeway because of fences and trees.

16. A property for which there is no immediate planned use.

17. Close to Social Services and to county government offices on Fair Lane

18. A convenient location for access by probation officers.

If, after a five-year lease, and the county has other uses for the property and wishes 30 have it returned, Hangtown Haven, Inc. will return it to its original condition.

Peter Wolfe, a licensed architect and a member of the advisory board of Hangtown Haven, Inc. has done the design. Note that each living space is the size of the mini buildings, most of which will initially be filled by tents.

Also enclosed is a five-page summary of the new organization of Hangtown Haven Inc. It is built upon an expanded Board of Directors that includes experts from Groen Valley Community Church. We feel that a larger board is necessary to provide the services and control necessary when the site is built and in operation. The summary also lists the members of the bom board, as they now exist.

In summary, the Board of Supervisors is not being asked to port El Dorado County in the homeless business. Rather it is being asked only to provide the property, as it did to United Outreach several years ago, so that Hangtown Haven, Ine. can provide a shelter to homeless residents. HTHI has the volunteers, skill and experience to make the Perks Court property a clean, safe and successful homeless encampment. It will provide El Dorado County homeless with a legal place to sleep, congregate, ent and will give them a chance for a new beginning in life. They will be encouraged to find work or higher education through living in the minibuildings and will not be allowed to panhandle tourists or congregate on the steps of local businesses. HTHI has proven its skill in designing and managing a vibrant encampment on Broadway in Placerville and will make Perks Court a successful example of how a community can deal with homelessness in a humane and effective way at no cost to the county. Few counties in California have stepped up to the challenge of homelessness. El Dorado County can take the lead.

Again, we ask only that the county grant IITHI a five-year lease of their property lot 32713019 on Perks Court on which we can build a homeless shelter initially consisting of tents and eventually mini-buildings along with two common area buildings. El Dorado County can be proud of its contribution to the safety and welfare of the homeless who live in our community.

Thank you very much. Sincerely,

Art Edwards, President Hangtown Haven, Inc.

The property on Perks Court described in the letter is adjacent to the property leased to United Outreach and is zoned "commercial" which permits a homeless shelter to be built on it by right. However, we were planning to start with individual tents until enough money could be raised to build the 8' x 12' buildings. Since tents are not permitted in any zone, it would have required a Special Use Permit to get started. Ast mentioned earlier, we have received no response to my letter from the supervisors since August of 2013.

Lot 32713019 Perks Court
Proposed New Homeless Shelter
Adjacent To Original Perks Court Property
Note Existing Concrete Slab For Common Area

I took the supervisor for that district, Brian Veeerkamp, on a tour of the property and showed him our plans and where everything would go. He seemed to be impressed, but nothing came of it. We have heard that the supervisors have been under heavy pressure from local businessınca to keep any homeless shelter out of that area. So far the supervisors have complied with that demand, and nothing has been built in the county to house the homeless.

In the late spring of 2014 the supervisors appointed a committee of "experience" homeless volunteers and city and county employees to work together to develop a homeless shelter and program for our county. This group, called the El Dorado County Homelessness Theory of Change (TC) Committee, meets periodically to talk about what to do for the homeless in

the county. It has been over a year now since it was organized, and phase two, the current phase is just beginning to discuss the possibility of a homeless shelter. It is estimated that agreement on a shelter, if it is ever reached, will happen in over a year from now.

People have complained that, while the committee is spending so much time getting "comensus" on the homeless issues, many people are freezing on the streets and in the hills around town. The county's response is that. "It is important to get community by- in through the consensus process before anything can get done to help the homeless." People who disagree with this process have said that. "No, all we need to get something done is for the supervisors to take a stand for the homeless." It is important to note that Only three of the committee members have ever built or operated a horseless shelter.

Not only has the Placerville City Council rejected any homeless shelter in the city. but the El Dorado Board of Supervisors will not even respond to my offer to build one in the county without taxpayer dollars.

Adjacent Counties

Because of the publicity we received, our name and accomplishments spread around the state. People from a number of counties visited us, toured the grounds and asked many questions. The question asked the most was, "How have you volunteers in El Dorado County done it and we haven't been able to? The following is some of the towns/counties whose representatives paid us a visit:

- Vallejo
- Garberville, Mendocino County

- Santa Cruz
- Stockton
- Sacramento
- Nevada City Auburn
- Grass Valley
- Marin County
- Eugene, Oregon
- Roseville

We also received donations and phone inquiries from San Antonio, Texas, Pennsylvania and New Jersey. Our fame and success bad spread across the country. Today, most of the cities counties listed above are designing as building homeless shelices based on our design and success. Our biggest claim to fanfic carte from the Los Angeles Times whose reporters and camera people traveled all the way from Los Angeles to do a story about us. But today, Efforts to help the homeless in El Dorado County are dormant.

Publicity

The issue of publicity is very important and should not be ignored. It seems intuitive that you should get all the publicity you can if you are building a homeless shelter. However, this is not always true. You need to think this one through completely before starting a publicity campaign.

It is natural to want to share your venture with local newspapers and TV stations. When you do, it is imperative that you share your intent with a paper or station that is sympathetic with your intentions. It is also important that your timing be

impeccable. We made a serious mistake on this final issue that I will now share with you.

I had made good preparations with our local paper for an article that would announce to the community our plans for a shelter. The article was written very well and it supported us completely. Unfortunately, the timing was terrible. The article alerted those who were opposed to our efforts before we had made significant progress on the project. It alerted our opposition and they mobilized quickly to do what they could to shut us down. There is an old saying that it is better to present your opposition with an accomplished fact than to alert them along the way. "It is better to ask for forgiveness than for permission," is very true when you are dealing with helping the homeless.

The good news about publicity is that it also alerts your supporters about what you are doing and can result in contributions. Channel 10 in Sacramento made a report on us interviewing me on site that made a lot of people mad but it also resulted in immediate contributions of over $1000 to our corporation. But it is a gamble, and the advantages and disadvantages must be weighed carefully before putting out any publicity about building a homeless shelter.

CHAPTER THIRTY

Health Connections House

Marshall Hospital has a large bill every year from the homeless population because every hospital in California is required by law to provide emergency medical care to anyone who comes into their emergency room either by ambulance or by car. The homeless people in our community recognize this and tend to take full advantage of it. When a homeless person has a splinter in his or her hand, he or she will often call an ambulance to take him to the hospital emergency room and get medical treatment. The hospital tells us that an ambulance trip to the emergency room costs around $12,000, and this cost, since the homeless person obviously cannot pay it, is spread around to everyone else's insurance. In other words, those of us who have insurance pay for the lack of a family doctor for the homeless.

This problem was alleviated by the existence of Hangtown Haven. We provided a doctor or nurse for each resident and would often drive the homeless to the emergency room if it was warranted, saving the hospital many thousand of dollars a year in unneeded emergency care. It always amazed me that the hospital didn't stand up and complain about the city's closing of the Haven. It should have been a simple economic issue with them.

To help solve this problem, Hangtown Haven, Ine. made a contract with Marshall Hospital through Partners in Care after the Haven was closed during the early spring of 2014. At the request of PIC, we leased a three bedroom home in the county, furnished it and set up a live-in manager. It was not easy to rent a home in which to house five otherwise homeless men and women, but the Reeder family wanted to do their bit for the homeless and gave us a good price to lease their home.

PIC established who would be a resident and for how long. These were homeless people who had had an operation but could not stay in the hospital any longer. Others needed care from the PIC nurse but didn't need hospital care

The Health Connections House was a huge success and saved the hospital a large amount of money. They told us that with only two residents in the home, the savings Exceeded their costs to keep it open. We were always provided free food by The Food Bark for the residents. The following is the summary of our guests in the Health Connections House for the year March 2014 through February 2015:

Total number of guests	23
Male	16
Female	7
Average stay per guest	27 days
Reason for using the house	
Recoup after hospitalization	20
Recovery after surgery	4
Mental Health	1
Physical rehab.	2
Housing during cancer treatment	2

Note: Some guests had more than one reason

Unfortunately, the hospital decided to end our contract after one year for what we heard were financial reasons and will now go back to providing "free" medical care to the homeless as the law requires.

When the hospital stopped funding our home, Partners in Care closed their doors and no longer exists. Community

Haven, Inc. then decided that the home was too good to let go. Consequently, we sat down with two other non-profit corporations in our community and negotiated a partnership that would utilize the home to help homeless people.

The three non-profits, Only Kindness (CRC), Community Haven, Inc. and Jobs Shelters of the Sierra (ISS) are now in partnership to keep the home going. Each has the following responsibilities:

- Community Haven, Inc. will maintain the home and pay the bills and will provide the house manager.
- Only Kindness (CRC) will select the homeless residents.
- JSS will utilize the garage for storing clothes, sleeping bags and tents for distribution to the homeless in the county.

This partnership has the distinction of being the first in our community in which three separate non-profits have joined together for the purpose of providing help to members of our homeless community. Each resident will be charged a nominal fee to live there. The fer will include food provided by the Food Bank and access to doctor's appointments provided by our van. The fees will not quite cover the cost of providing and maintaining the home, so we are looking for financial help from other non-profits or generous individuals. This arrangement by the three non-profits holds the possibility of things to come. Hopefully the county will see this us a positive sign for providing help for our homeless,

It isn't as much as we would like to do or are capable of doing, but In the meantime, we will do what we can with what is available. If you want to dig through a mountain and the only tool you have is a spoon, start digging.

Health Connections House Now Home For Four Homeless Persons Jobs Shelters of The Sierra

My good friend Ron Sachs founded John's Shelters of The Sierra (ISS) several years ago. It has been his intention to provide the needs of the homeless by distributing clothes, sleeping bugs, tents and sundries in his car several times a week. His group has expanded into a successful non-profit corporation now with many volunteers making the rounds of the known homeless areas several times a week. They distribute toilet paper, socks, underwear, and all kinds of other clothing, tents and sleeping bags.

Unfortunately, the volunteers have been experiencing some of the harassment that is outlined in the next chapter and they are becoming afraid to continue. The police haven't arrested anyone yet, but no one wants to make the police angry.

We have just heard that a Placerville police car drove up to the JSS van recently and the policeman told the volunteer to stop passing out clothes to the homeless. The cop said that the

businesses. in the area are complaining that the customers are reluctant to shop in an area in which homeless are congregating and waiting for the JSS van to deliver much needed clothes and sundries. The location in question is in the parking lot in front of the Dollar Store adjacent to the road on the outside of the parking area.

Our lawyer tells us that there is nothing we can do to prevent police harassment. They appear to be immune from complaints that they are going beyond the law even though there is no law keeping volunteers from passing out clothes in a parking lot. What kind of a country do we want to live in, where the police make the law?

CHAPTER THIRTY-ONE

Food For The Hungry

For many years a church-based organization (FAITH) has been providing lunches for the homeless people of our community. In addition, food has been available for years at the Upper Room where a free dinner is provided every night beginning at 4:00 PM for anyone who comes in. Volunteers run the Upper Room and its food comes from the Food Bank. It has been very successful but provides everyone only one meal a day. Nothing was available for lunch until the churches got together and organized volunteers to prepare and deliver lunches around the community.

The lunch program has been successful for ten years or so in the community. The FAITH organization has taken it over and their volunteers are out every day in their vars delivering sandwiches, chili or lasagna at various meeting points around the city and county. The homeless typically know where the food car will be and congregate there at noon every day.

This arrangement had worked very well until recently when the police apparently decided to step in. One place in the city limits had been a large congregating area for noontime food distribution. There is a motel on the east end of town in which homeless people can stay at a low price. It is near an adjacent forest where many homeless live. I have seen over forty homeless gather in the hotel's parking lot waiting for the noontime food delivery by the FAITH volunteers. The motel owners didn't mind and there were no neighbors close by to comment, so it went on for years.

The police apparently decided to put a stop to food delivery at this morel, but they had a problem. People can do anything they want on their owa property as long as it's not breaking a law, and there is no law saying that you can't feed someone on

your property. So the police could not stop them, but they were not to be deterred. I will repeat the next few paragraphs as the story was told to me by several reliable sources since I was not present.

One day at noon, the homeless were gathered in the motel parking lot when a city police car drove up and a uniformed cop went out. She asked to speak to the motel manager. He came out of his office and asked what she wanted. She is reported to have said, "I would like you to stop feeding the homeless on your property." The manager seemed to have his wits about him when he apparently responded, "By law, you cannot stop us and I cannot make that decision, I am only the manager. Only the owner can make that decision."

With apparent irritation in her voice she is reported to have asked, "Where do I find the owner?" The manager replied that he is in the office.

"Thank you," she said and then walked into the motel office alone. Several minutes passed, and the policeman walked out of the office, climbed into her police car and drove off. Shortly after, the motel owner walked out of his office into the parking lot and said in a shaken voice that, "I am sorry but you will all have to leave. We no longer will be allowing lunch to be distributed on this property."

I was not present at this gathering nor did I personally hear any of the conversation that I've reported. However, I refer to it as a fact since the people who were delivering the food had arrived shortly after the police car drove up. These events have also been. confirmed to me by several homeless who were present at the exchange.

We have heard since then that when city council members are asked why they shut down this feeding location at the motel, the standard answer is, "Oh we didn't do that. The motel owner

decided that he didn't want them around any more and shut it down himself."

The motel owner had been allowing and encouraging volunteers to provide and distribute lunches in this parking lot for at least the ten years that I have been active in helping the homeless. And suddenly after a policeman has a five-minute conversation with the owner, he changes his mind and prohibits homeless from being fed on his property? I won't speculate further but will allow the reader to draw his/her own conclusions.

There is now no place in the city where you can feed homeless people without being hassled by the police. In fact, the city has ruled that homeless cannot congregate in the one city park called Lumsden. In summary, there is no place to sleep. sit in a pack of bud lite beaches, get clothes, tents or sleeping bags, get delivered food, get free medical care, pentanile, go to the bathroom (with one exception) or sit on the sidewalk without risk of being arrested. I have heard it said that city employees have boasted that "We will make it so miserable for them that soon all the homeless will be run out of Placerville." Our tax money is paying for people who seem to be well on their way to doing just that. In summary, in Placerville it is illegal to:

Feed the homeless on private property Pander or ask for money.

Feed the hungry or the streets.

Give the homeless clothes in parking lots. Sleep anywhere in town.

Congregate in the city park during the day.

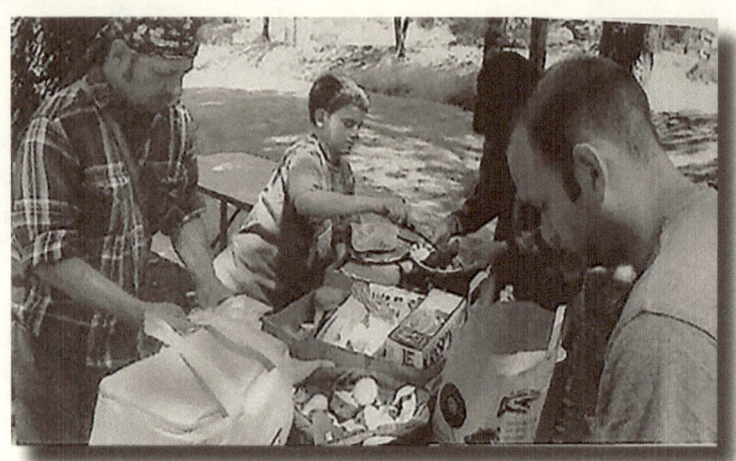

Author's Grandson, Conner Edwards, Feeding Chile To The Homeless

**Volunteers Distributing Sleeping Bags in Lumsden Park
Before Being Shut Down**

CHAPTER THIRTY-TWO

A Happy Ending

During the spring of 2015, two of the original members of the Hangtown Haven council were married at Federated Church. Becky and Ken had fallen in love during the operation of the Haven and finally decided that it was time to tie the knot.

It was a spectacular wedding with many they had met on their way out of homelessness invited including the ex-mayor and her husband. When the Haven closed down, Becky went to work as office manager at a local automobile repair shop, and Ken and James (best man) joined together to form a handyman home repair service. As of this writing, Those Guys, the name of their company, is booked out for two months and Becky is running the auto shop like a pro.

They all live in homes now and are doing very well. Becky invited me to be her father and walk her down the aisle. This experience was most exciting for me since it will be the only time I get to be the father of the bride since both of my daughters have died in the past ten years. My wife, Shirley, was asked to be the mother of the bride and she gladly accepted. James Adkins was Ken's best man and Bruce Lacher was his groomsman. Becky's maid of honor was her daughter, Sierra Nylunder and her bridesmaid was Sonni Gill.

Ken Burkey officiated as the pastor and Ron Sachs was the celebrant. Ken is the pastor at Green Valley Church but that church doesn't do weddings so Andrew Headden, the pastor at Federated, graciously allowed Pastor Burkey to perform the wedding at our church.

When the bride and I stepped into the chapel arm in arm the crowd of friends and relatives sitting in the pews jumped to

their feet clapping, whistling and cheering. It was an amazing experience to see how far these two previously homeless people had come from the day they walked into the Haven looking sad, lost and afraid. It is a good example of what can be accomplished by homeless people when they are given a place to live and a hand up. Becky tells everyone who will listen that Hangtown Haven saved her life. Just think how many more lives could have been saved and turned around had the Haven been allowed to continue.

Becky and Ken Get Married

The Author, Bruce Lacher, Shirley Edwards

James Adkins, Ken Green and Bruce Lacher

The Wedding Party

CHAPTER THIRTY-THREE

Ninth Circuit Court of Appeals

Citing sweeping, venerable core case law on the civil rights of individuals in public places, the Ninth Circuit on June 19, 2014 overturned Los Angeles' Municipal Code Sec. 85.02 statute against use of vehicles for habitation.

The ruling in Desertrain v. City of Los Angeles potentially reduces city government control over the uses and appearance of public spaces. On the other hand it enhances the ability of people who have lost conventional housing to use their vehicles for some of the purposes of a home, rather than face the riskier, more stereotypically "homeless" situations of lugging possessions by hand on city streets or relying fully on institution shelters and services.

The Ninth Circuit opinion, written by Judge Harry Pregerson, found the Los Angeles ordinance unconstitutionally vague on the grounds that "Plaintiffs are left guessing as to what behavior would subject them to citation and arrest by an officer," and that the ordinance encouraged arbitrary and discriminatory enforcement against homeless people.

The opinion reviewed the circumstances of four plaintiffs cited and arrested for allegedly living in their cars during a Venice-area enforcement campaign in fall 2010. (Seven plaintiffs are named in the caption, but a footnote explains that some received parking tickets while parked with disability placards, and the parties agreed those tickets were a mistake.)

In all of the described cases, the cited parties kept possessions in their vehicles, but two slept in their vehicles at night only while parked on private property by permission. A third, warmed against sleeping in his car, "then began sleeping on the sidewalk, which is legal," and at times slept in a shelter. The

fourth, when arrested, insisted he was not sleeping, but was told, "that sleeping is not the only criteria for violating Section 85.02.

The opinion further recounted evidence of conflicting understandings among city officers about the meaning of the ordinance. It said that while legitimate health and safety issues were raised about the conditions in which vehicle campers were living. "some of the conduct plaintiffs were engaged in when arrested -- eating, talking on the phone, or escaping the rain in their vehicles - mimics the everyday conduct of many Los Angeles residents."

It concluded that the law is so vague that it fails to give notice of the conduct it actually prohibits," and as interpreted by city police, was "incompatible with the concept of un evenhanded administration of the law to the poor and to the rich that is fundamental to a democratic society."

The opinion quoted at length from Papachristou v. City of Jacksonville, the exceptionally literary 1970 Supreme Court opinion by Justice William O. Douglas that overturned, us void for vagueness, old-style vagrancy laws that formerly authorized arrest for slatuses such as unemployment and for ill-defined offenses such as "loitering".

Judges Marsha S. Berzon and Morgan Christen joined Pregerson in the opinion. Their decision overturned a 2011 district court ruling that had backed the city and arrested officers in cross-motions for summary judgment. As a threshold matter, the Ninth Circuit found it proper to consider the plaintiffs' vagueness challenge to the ordinance, raised in the Plaintiffs' motion, although they did not raise the vagueness aspect of their constitutional argument until after filing their first amended complaint. The local district court had refused to consider the merits of the vagueness challenge.

Mark Ryavec, head of the Venice Stakeholders Association, and a campaigner against campers on Venice streets, complained to the Los Angeles Times, "It leaves people who are mentally ill, criminally inclined or lethal on your doorstep and removes any possibility the police can do anything about it."

The decision does not necessarily grant blanket permission to sleep in vehicles in all circumstances. Vehicular residents are potentially affected by many laws, including parking restrictions, vehicle codes, and disorderly-conduct statutes that prohibit many kinds of living activities on public property. It remains to be seen how much Desertrain may hold back the use of such additional measures.

However, the case has already been recognized as having important effects throughout California. William Abrams, a consulting professor at Stanford who has represented vehicular residents in Palo Alto, told a local paper he thought the holding "will apply completely if we were to have to go to court" over Palo Alto's ordinance against vehicle sleeping.

Activist attorney Carol Sobel, who represented the plaintiffs, told the KPCC radio station that since her clients did not sleep in their vehicles on public property, the case for them was principally about the ability to use vehicles on a public street in the daytime without being singled out for having certain kinds of property in their vehicles. She said in the radio interview that all four of her clients had been arrested under the invalidated statute, which was defined as a misdemeanor, and two lost their vehicles to towing. Asked whether tolerating vehicle habitation created sanitation concerns, or whether it reduced pressure to provide real housing, she said the answer to needs for sanitation and for housing wasn't to put people in jail.

Los Angeles City Attorney Mike Feuer told the press he would not appeal the decision but would seek to redraft the

ordinance instead. He told the LA Times, "We need to take a break from the past... and commit ourselves to grappling with the issues that create homelessness in the first place."

Thank God for the Ninth Circuit Court of Appeals! It's unconstitutional to ban the homeless from sleeping outside, the federal government says

That we all need sleep is a fact of life but also a legally important point. Last week, the Department of Justice argued as much in a statement of interest it titled in a relatively obscure case in Boise, Idaho, that could impact how entities regulate and punish homelessness.

Boise, like many cities the number of which has swelled since the recession- has an ordinance banning sleeping or camping in public places. But such laws, the DOJ says, effectively criminalize homelessness itself in situations where people simply have nowhere else to sleep.

When adequate shelter space exists, individuals have a choice about whether or not to sleep in public. However, when adequate shelter space does not exist, there is no meaningful distinction between the status of being homeless and the conduct of sleeping in public. Sleeping is a life-sustaining activity-ie, it must occur at some time in some place. If a person literally has nowhere else to go, then enforcement of the anti-camping ordinance against that person criminalizes her for being homeless.

Such laws, the DOJ argues, violate the Eighth Amendment protections against cruel and unusual punishment, making them unconstitutional. By weighing in on this case. The DOJ's find foray in two decades into this still-unsettled area of law,

the federal government is warning cities far beyond Boise and backing up federal goals to treat homelessness more humanely.

"It's huge," says Eric Tars, a senior attorney for the National Law Center on Homelessness & Poverty, which originally filed the lawsuit against Roise, alongside Idaho Legal Aid Services. (Lifting bans on sleeping outside won't stop criminalization of homelessness] According to a NLCHP report last year that surveyed 187 cities between 2011 and 2014, 34 percent had citywide laws banning camping in public. Another 43 percent prohibited sleeping in vehicles, and 53 percent based sitting or lying down in certain public places. All of these laws criminalize the kind of activities - sitting, resting, and sleeping that are arguably fundamental to human existence.

They've criminalized that behavior in an environment where most cities have far more homeless people than shelter beds. In 2014, the federal government estimates, there were about 153,000 unsheltered homeless on the street in the U.S. on any given night. Laws like these have grown more common as homelessness has actually grown worse since the recession.

"Homelessness is just becoming more visible in communities, and when homelessness becomes more visible, there's more pressure on community leaders to do something about it," Tars says. "And rather than actually exploring what's the best thing to do about homelessness, the knee-jerk response as with so many other things in society is 'we'll address this social issue within the criminal justice system."

It's also easier, he adds, for elected officials to argue for criminal penalties when the public costs of that policy are much harder to see than the costs of investing in shelters. or services for the poor. Ultimately, though, advocates and the federal government have argued, it's much more expensive to ticket the homeless with the court, prison and health costs associated with

it than to invest in "housing first" solutions that have worked in many parts of the country.

Criminal citations also compound the problem of homelessness, making it harder for people to qualify for jobs or housing in the future.

"You have to check those [criminal] boxes on the application forms," Tours says, "and they don't say 'were you arrested because you were trying to simply survive on the streets?" They say "if you have an arrest record, we're not going to rent to you."

NLCHP's ghoul, Tars says, isn't to protect the rights of people living on the street, but to prevent and end homelessness. That means adding a lot more shelter beds and housing options in places like Boise which has three shelters run by two nonprofits so people have options other than the street.

The DOJ's argument is based on the logic in an earlier Ninth Circuit decision, striking down vagrancy law in Los Angeles that was ultimately vacated it a settlement. That logic specifically says it's unconstitutional to punish people for sleeping outside if there aren't enough beds for them to sleep indoors. If there were, the constitutional question would be different, although the moral and policy implications may remain the same.

"Homelessness never left town because somebody gave it a ticket," Tars says. "The only way to end homelessness is to make sure everybody has access to affordable, decent housing." It appears that this U.S. Department of Justice is getting involved in homelessness for the first in our history. The DOJ's opinion is just that, an opinion, until a court rules. But it's a start, and maybe cities and counties will soon be required to provide shelters for their homeless populations. It is not likely to happen in my lifetime, but I think it is inevitable.

Maybe I'll be back in my next life in time to help.

CHAPTER THIRTY-FOUR

In Conclusion

As of now, the spring of 2016, there is no homeless shelter either in El Dorado County or in the City of Placerville that is capable of housing forty homeless people for twenty-four hours a day. There are various private homes in the area that have been rented for the homeless, but they will hold a maximum of only six people per property by law. In addition, the Nomad Rotating Shelter program started on November 1" and will close by April 1". but it is only open at night. It is just as cold and wet during the day.

The county's Theory of Change committee is working on getting consensus to build some type of facility, but that project is at least a year away, maybe two. Community Haven, Inc. (previously Hangtown Haven) has offered to build a shelter that could hold up to a hundred homeless at no cost to the taxpayer, but the county has ignored us, while saying that they will contribute nothing to a homeless shelter. So we continue to search for financial and political support that will allow us to build a shelter somewhere in El Dorado County in spite of the opposition from some of the powerful leaders in our community.

It is indeed a thrill to see the successful transition of these formerly homeless people into productive lives. This all came about in no small part because we were allowed to build a homeless shelter in our community. One can't help but wonder how many more success stories I could tell if the mayor and city council had allowed us to keep Hangtown Haven in operation.

In looking back on the shelter, I have concluded that the success of the Haven was due mostly to an unusual confluence of dedicated people. Each one did his or her share to make it a success and all were available at just the right time. Here is a

list of them alphabetically and their jobs as I remember each. I apologize to anyone I've inadvertently left out.

- Larry Allum, Ken Green, James Adkins, Becky Nylander Green, Frank MatousHomeless members, HTH resident council
- Mike Applegarth -County employee
- Carl Bialorucki-Sergeant Placerville Police Department
- Tim Bailey-Electrical contractor
- Ken Burkey Head Pastor GVCC
- Janis and Tom Carney-Volunteers
- Marie Cook CRC
- Jim Ellsworth - Secretary/Treasurer HTHI
- Jeff England - El Dorado Disposal
- Rene Evans - CRC
- Bruce Lacher - Fire Chief, board member HTHI
- Dave Machado - Placerville City Council and volunteer
- Laurie Marchant Health Coordinator
- Cleve Morris - Placerville City Manager
- George Neilson Placerville Chief of Police
- Don Rake-Volunteer coordinator, board member HTHI Russ and Rob Reod-Heavy equipment operators
- Ron Sachs-Vice President HTHI, President JSS
- Cyndy Salmon-HTIII Board of Directors Wendy Schultz- Reporter Mt. Democrat
- Steve Stockwell Volunteer

- Wendy Thomas - Vice Mayor, Mayor, City Council Member
- Don Vanderkar-Vice President HTHI
- Ron Wells Wells Automotive
- Barry Wilkinson HTH Property owner
- Wilkinson Portable Toilets, Inc.

There are those who have told me that my name belongs on this list, so here it is:

- Art Edwards - President United Outreach, President, CEO, Community (previously Hangtown) Haven, Inc.

The preceding list includes only those people directly associated with the success of Hangtown Haven as remembered by the author. It does not include the names of the many volunteers who have worked tirelessly to provide food and over night shelter to the other homeless in our community. To these dedicated citizens I offer my thanks and hope for future success. I would attempt to list the ones with whom I am familiar, but I would certainly leave some out resulting in confusion and resentment. Keep it up guys!

In reviewing this chapter I realize that I have left out the special contribution made by the Mountain Democrat reporter, Wendy Schultz. She visited the shelter periodically and interviewed many of its residents. She also interviewed me on several occasions, and her articles were accurate and comprehensive. I always thanked her for her articles and interest in our attempts to help the homeless and still consider her to be a good personal friend.

We have just heard that our new chief of police has fired our wonderful policeman Sergeant Carl Bialorucky, who was in

charge of the Hangtown Haven area on Upper Broadway under Chief Neilson and one of the best on the force. Curl was known for treating homeless people with respect and consideration. The rumors are flying in the homeless community but we don't know exactly why he was fired. We can only guess, but it seems to be pretty obvious. I am sure that the city will not tell us, probably claiming that it is a "personnel" matter. Is our police force required to harass the homeless under threat of dismissal?

We are now hearing about the town of Flint, Michigan, that has been dealt a serious health blow by a conservative governor who decided to switch their water supply from a very clean source to a virtual sewer filled with garbage and contaminants. It is contaminated with lead and other heavy metals that have a serious health effect on children. The Governor did this in order to save a few dollars each year so that he could give the wealthy taxpayers in the state a generous tax break. The residents of Flint are poor, disadvantaged and live in down and out poverty. In other words, they have no political power or influence in their government's operation.

The culture in Flint sounds very much like the homeless culture we see here in California. The way that Flint residents have been treated sounds very much like the way the homeless are treated every day here in Placerville and El Dorado County. The poor in Michigan and the homeless in California are treated very much alike, and that won't change as long as politicians in power care more for their bottom line profit than they do about the lives of poor, disadvantaged Americans. Poor people all over the country are being treated the same way.

Chances are slim that we will be able to build a homeless shelter in the county or city during my lifetime (I am 83). A majority of our reigning politicians will have to be turned out of office before that happens. So the community is left with powerful people who our elected officials are reluctant to anger.

We are reminded that three new members of the Board of Supervisors have recently been elected, and two more are leaving the city council soon so there may be a change coming. But nothing that would help the homeless population has surfaced yet.

I apologize to those homeless who were living at Hangtown Haven when the city closed it down. I tried with everything I had to keep it open, to provide shelter for forty otherwise homeless people, but I failed. The toughest part of the whole process was the realization that many residents were on the road to addiction recovery but were forced back out onto the streets and forest to sleep alone resulting in their return to addiction.

Ron Sachs and his JSS volunteers are still providing tents, clothes and sleeping bags, but the lives the homeless are now forced to live does not compare to what they had at the Haven. If we had done something differently, if I had better political skills, maybe they would still be in their home on Broadway. Who knows?

The King Arthur legend tells us that, yes, once upon a time there was a Camelot. from July of 2012 to November of 2013. It was a miracle that no one thought would work, but it did.

Today when you wander over the deserted site on upper Broadway that was once Hangtown Haven and listen carefully, you can almost hear the happy voices of people who had once lost everything but were working hard toward recovery. You can hear the voices of women who, for the first time in their lives, felt secure and protected from sexual attack, who could now hug a stranger while sharing affection that had previously eluded them. You hear men laughing and sharing stories around the warm campfire, stories of how they are pulling out of addiction and preparing to return to the community. You can hear policemen, led by their chief, joking and sharing food and

coffee with men and women who were once terrified of just seeing a policeman approach them. You can almost see men and women working to help each other and gathering food to deliver to people who were worse off than they.

I do not consider myself qualified to judge others on what motivates their actions. Each one of us must answer for his/her own behavior. Hopefully, each member of the city council and the county board of supervisors will have to explain why they did not allow forty or more homeless men and women to live peacefully and happily in a safe shelter at no cost to the taxpayer. I would like to be there when Saint Peter asks each of them, "Why did you close down a successful shelter in the middle of winter and forest forty of God's people to live on the streets and in the forest?" Maybe I will learn something I don't know.

We will not give up! Maybe a sugar daddy with a million dollars will come along and give us a used, some property or a building. It is not likely, but sometimes all you have left is hope. Just to see the success of broken people rise out of the ashes of despair and addiction and return to a normal life has been more than worth it. As my mother, who grew up dirt poor in Western Colorado, used to tell her son during the depression;

"Don't fail to help anyone in need, Art, whether you think they deserve it or not."

Alice Marie Rice Echwards

Sorry mom. I tried my best.

Camelot Returned To Nature

EPILOGUE

This is a true story told, as the author remembers it, with no attempt to protect the identity of the participants. At this time, it appears futile to attempt to build a homeless shelter of any kind in either the City of Placerville or in el Dorado County. The power structure will not permit it, even though it would cost the taxpayer nothing. It is hoped, however, that the lessons learned can be applied in other communities around the nation, so that homeless, somewhere, can be given another shot at life. If even a few can be helped, this book will be worth the effort.

As of the late fall of 2015, we applied for a grant from the El Dorado Community Foundation here in Placerville. The director, Bill Roby just wrote me that they would not be giving us the grant I applied for that would have kept open the Women's Shelter in Diamond Springs. The Community Foundation has not been generous with grains to us since we opened in 2012. Of the $60K or so that we have received in gifts and grants since then, the Foundation has given us only $250. However, we recently received a grant of $500 from an individual member of the Community Foundation.

Bill has recently told us that they would not be giving any grants to Hangtown Haven, Inc. in the foreseeable future. I have no idea why they will not help us support the homeless. The members of the Foundation are all wealthy residents of the county so I should have been prepared for rejection. Somewhere along the line we must have angered them maybe by building a successful shelter on Upper Broadway. The bottom line is that, without financial support, our days of helping the homeless are now numbered and we will have to shut down our non-profit corporation in a few months. Maybe then I could really retire. However, I would much rather be helping the homeless.

A VERY HAPPY ENDING

Since Hangtown Haven was closed down in 2013, we have been working with the El Dorado Board of Supervisors to fund a county-wide homeless shelter in or near the city of Placerville. We were unsuccessful until two things happened: one, the county moved the kids out of juvenile hall leaving it completely empty, and two, the election of the ex-mayor of Placerville, Wendy Thomas, to the Board of Supervisors. With an empty juvie sitting in Placerville, and Wendy Thomas, and homeless supervisor supporter, John Hidahl on the board, they supported our call to house up to sixty homeless men and women getting them off of the street and into a warm building with showers, kitchen, meeting rooms, TV, laundry room, air conditioning, heating, basketball court and dining hall. All of this is funded by the State of California and operated by Volunteers of America.

We have many more than 60 homeless in El Dorado County, so the county is moving onto the next phase. The sheriff's department has moved out of their old building and into a new one designed strictly for law enforcement, leaving an empty lot on county property. As I write this, the county engineering department is designing a new building on the old sheriff's property to house several hundred homeless in a building of their own in a couple of years.

It has taken years and continual dedication by a group of homeless advocates led by a retired aerospace engineer supported by the city mayor (now county supervisor) and many volunteers. It was all shown that it could be done when we built Hangtown Haven ten years ago. Someday I want to write a book describing our a new homeless shelter designed to give hundreds of our neighbors their own place to live that is off the streets and out of the forest. Then I can retire.